Learn

Me

Gooder

Learn Me Gooder is available online at Amazon (print and Kindle), Barnes and Noble (print and Nook), the iPad store, and smashwords.

I invite you to follow me on any or all of the following internet media:

Blog – http://www.learnmegood.com
Facebook – http://www.facebook.com/learnmegood
Twitter – @learnmegood
Email – learnmegood2@yahoo.com

ISBN713: 978-1463794002
ISBN-10: 1463794002

*I dedicate this book to my blushing bride,
the love of my life*

Introduction

When I first published Learn Me Good, I had no idea how successful it would be. Sure, in my daydreams, it would become an international bestseller, I'd receive multiple invitations to appear on Oprah's show, and every house would have 2 copies (one for each bathroom). Realistically though, I figured most of my friends and family would feel obligated to buy a copy, and anything beyond that would be gravy.

Instead, I was shocked – pleasantly so, not hit with a taser – at how many people genuinely embraced Learn Me Good, recommended it to friends and colleagues, and even clamored for a sequel. Many of these readers discovered LMG through the rise of e-readers, most notably the Kindle, to which I may owe my first-born child.

I actually started working on this sequel, Learn Me Gooder, back in 2006, right after LMG came out. I worked on it a little bit here, a little bit there, yet something always sidetracked me. School, television, then a girlfriend, who became a fiancée, who turned into a wife.

Finally, I buckled down and got serious in August of 2010. I figured if the world really IS going to end in 2012, and that Mayan prophecy isn't just some time-traveler's idea of a practical joke, I ought to have at least one more grammatically incorrect title out and available.

While I'm on the subject of the title, I knew pretty early on that I was going to go with Learn Me Gooder. Still, that didn't stop me from considering a few Hollywood-inspired sequel subtitles. Here's a small sampling of the list I came up with:

Learn Me Good 2: Academic Boogaloo
Learn Me Good 2: Marvin's Revenge
Learn Me Good 2: Learn Harder
Learn Me Good 2: The Temple of Gloom
Learn Me Good 2: A Fistful of Dawdlers
Learn Me Good 2: The Fellowship of the Bling
Learn Me Good 2: The Engineer Strikes Back
Learn Me Good 2: The Math of Khan

In the end, I decided simpler was better, and Learn Me Gooder was my final answer.

Just like the first time around, Learn Me Gooder is mostly based on real experiences, but they have been embellished, fictionalized, and condensed into a single school year. All of the names have once again been changed to protect the innocent, the red-handed, and the apathetic.

Six years have passed since the events of Learn Me Good, and Jack Woodson is still sharing stories and insights through emails with his friend and former colleague Fred Bommerson, who works at Heat Pumps Unlimited, Jack's old employer. Much like the recurring Death Star, the TAKS, or Texas Assessment of Knowledge and Skills, still looms over Jack's head.

One more time, I feel the need to stress that this book is a work of fiction. A few of the Amazon reviews for Learn Me Good took ME to task for the acts of Mr. Woodson. One review even began – "Appalling treatment of endangered children!"

I would ask everyone reading this to keep in mind that certain stories have been altered, supplemented, or even completely made up, and that I myself did not actually do every single thing that Jack Woodson does in the book. For instance, on page 98, where Mr. Woodson throws lemon meringue pies at the kids every time they tell him there are 365 days in a week – I never actually did that in my class.

In a similar vein, my wife, upon whom the character "Jill" is based, insisted that I state that there was not nearly so much drama during our actual courtship. Lucky for me.

Finally, I want to send big thanks out to several people. To my family and friends for helping me through this writing process and for being so supportive. To my friend and colleague Michael J. Ruiz for his contribution of the sign-off name used on the October 12 email. To Xavier Rodriguez for the use of his classroom and chalkboard which appear on the cover, to Shawn Fernandez for taking the pictures, and to my nephew Ethan for joining me as a cover model. To Carley Barnes for cover concept ideas, and to Terry Roy for finalizing those cover ideas.

Thanks for reading, and enjoy the story!

John Pearson   July, 2011

Date: Monday, August 24, 2009
To: Fred Bommerson
From: Jack Woodson
Subject: Here we go again

Fred! My man!

Long time no talk, buddy! Wait, I talked to you on Saturday, right? But it's been a long time since I e-mailed you from my classroom! What's that you say – I've NEVER e-mailed you from my classroom? That's because the portable classrooms outside didn't have Internet access, but this year – wait for it – I'm inside the main building, baby!

I'm very pleased to report that the third grade will no longer be treated like steerage on the Titanic! No more sloshing through puddles when it rains just to get to the cafeteria. No more braving the freezing cold in February during rest-room breaks. No more families of raccoons living (and sometimes dying) underneath the classroom floor.

Being inside will be fantastic. But I have so much more to talk about than just the new digs. Today was the first day of the brand new school year, and it's amazing how I still get the first-day jitters, even with seven years of experience under my belt. I got into bed at ten o'clock last night, but I know I didn't fall asleep before two. When I DID sleep, I had dreams where I was in class but couldn't talk. When I opened my mouth, all that came out was a bleating trumpet sound, a la Charlie Brown's generic adult. Not a very restful night, but I was up and at the school at seven anyway, ready and raring to go.

My morning started in the moshpit of our gymnasium, where all of the students and most of their parents had been packed in like sardines, waiting for the teachers to pick up their classes. I waded in to the gym, and it occurred to me that I must not be doing things right as a teacher because every year, they send me brand new kids and tell me to start over!

As I made my way through the maddening crowd, one lady stopped me and asked, "Excuse me, are you Mr. Woodson? Do you have Lakeisha Jefferson in your class?"

I consulted my class roster, and sure enough, there she was. Upon hearing the news, Ms. Jefferson seemed pleased that I would be teaching her daughter. A little TOO pleased. After witnessing a lengthy victory dance and the fourth violent hip thrust, I was starting to feel slightly uncomfortable with just HOW pleased she seemed to be.

She explained, "Lakeisha can be a handful sometimes, but I think she'll behave better for a male teacher."

Oh, joy! That's a theory I can't WAIT to test!

Once I had rounded up my students and taken them to my classroom, I was able to observe a few of the other kids. I have a boy named Jacob who is only 7 years old. Typically, third graders begin the year at age 8 and turn 9 at some point. Sure, we get our fair share of retainees who turn 10 (or, in one or two instances, 11) years old in the third grade. And I'm not even counting Alhambra, who turned 16, because he was clearly at the wrong school. But Jacob will only TURN 8 this year! He's a baby among babies! He does seem relatively bright, though.

On the other end of the spectrum, we have Nestor (already 9 years old), who can barely read or write. He already has me extremely worried.

This morning, I started the kids off with the usual first day activities – partial differential equations. Just kidding, they were doing the simple little "tell me about yourself" worksheets. Favorite color, favorite movies, names of family members, etc. I noticed Nestor following a pattern. He would ask his neighbor, "What does this say?" Then he would scribble something on his paper. "What does this say?" Scribble.

I wandered over and glanced at his paper. On every line, he had written the same thing, which was not even a real word.

"What is your favorite book?"
"OGO"
"How many brothers and sisters do you have?"
"OGO"
"What is your best friend's name?"
"OGO"

Clearly, I was not going to glean any personal information from Nestor's entrance questionnaire. So I decided to use an alternate assessment to gauge his number sense. I gave him a blank sheet of paper and asked him to write down the numbers in order, as high as he could count. I watched as he wrote 1, 2, and 3, then I walked away to see how some of the other kids were doing. After about three minutes, Nestor raised his hand and motioned me over.

He asked, "What comes after R?"

At that moment, I experienced an ice cream headache without having actually consumed any ice cream.

As you can see, I've got my work cut out for me here. Nestor's counting woes already make me think back to Hernando from a few years ago, who ALWAYS thought "catorce" came next when counting. Whenever we had a little free time, we would break out the counting cubes and practice in his native language.

"Uno, dos, tres. . . What comes next, Hernando?"

"Catorce?"

It's possible that Bono of U2 was hanging around my portable that year and used Hernando as an inspiration for the opening to "Vertigo," but somehow I doubt it.

There are two girls named Anna in my homeroom this year. They're quite easy to tell apart, though. One of them is super short, and the other has an unusually deep, raspy voice. Both seem intelligent and well behaved, so I'm pleased to have both "Tiny Anna" and "Smoker Anna" in my class.

My afternoon class started the day in Mrs. Bird's classroom (she's my partner this year). One of her introductory activities was having the kids write their answer to the question, "How did you spend your summer?"

I looked at a random paper this afternoon, from a little girl named Betsy, and I was pleased to see that it started with, "It was fun, we went to Six Flags and Cici's Pizza, and I got a new puppy."

That's so much better than if it had said, "My dad got caught trying to smuggle illegal fighting llamas into the country, so we visited him every Thursday from two to four at the Brownsville County Lockup. Also, my new puppy smells like paint thinner."

Another girl in Mrs. Bird's homeroom already feels comfortable enough to use a nickname in class. Her name is Gwenn, but on her papers, she wrote "Priti Prinses." I'm assuming she means Pretty Princess. I'm also assuming that's a self-appointed nickname.

Well hey, I think the custodians want me out of here now, so I'm going to go home and find something to eat. Say hey to the gang there at Heat Pumps Unlimited for me. Let them know that my days of sleeping till noon are over.

At least until Saturday.

Talk to you later,

Newt B Ginnings

Date: Wednesday, August 26, 2009
To: Fred Bommerson
From: Jack Woodson
Subject: The leg bone's connected to the... elbow?

Hey Fred,

I find it oddly kind of sweet that Larry has been looking forward to my first message, but that still doesn't give him the right to open your email when you're not around. Even if he IS your supervisor now. And I STILL don't understand how that happened.

But hey, him being a bonehead transitions nicely into my first story today.

As part of the first lesson in science class, we've begun to explore different examples of systems. Today, we took a look at the human skeleton. The kids partnered up, and I gave each pair a skeleton puzzle. There were about twenty pieces to each skeleton, some representing individual bones and some depicting sets of bones like the ribcage. The kids used brads to connect the bones through holes in each piece.

Let me tell you, my kids have some VERY convoluted ideas about how their bodies are put together.

One group immediately tried to fasten the pelvis to the base of the skull. Every group in my afternoon class thought that the arm only had one bone, so they had the hand approximately where the elbow should be. The part of the spinal column that was supposed to go between the rib cage and the pelvis was instead placed by one group on the underside of the pelvis. I didn't have the heart, or the guts, to tell them that there is actually no bone there.

The skeletons weren't the only things not making sense today. Class sizes have gotten a bit uneven. On Monday, I had 13 kids in my class. My other class, Mrs. Bird's homeroom, had 12. The other four third grade classes had similar numbers.

Today, I have 20 students in my homeroom. Mrs. Bird has 14, and the closest other class has 15. For some reason, our enrollment person, Mrs. O'Reilly, keeps depositing all of the new third graders into my homeroom!

This might not be so bad if they came bearing gifts of frankincense and myrrh, but most of them haven't even borne pencils or notebooks.

Maybe Mrs. O'Reilly is sending so many students to me because I'm the grade chair this year. This means I get to keep track of things for the grade level and be responsible for receiving and passing on information from the administration. And this year, grade chair is an unpaid position! Woohoo! This is of course why I have the honor of serving in this capacity. The third grade team was asked to choose someone, a vigorous game of rock-paper-scissors ensued, and my strategy of "always go paper" did not serve me well.

But at any rate, even with all of the new kids coming to me, I can be thankful that one holy terror was already firmly planted in another third grade class. His name is Roy'al, which is ironic, because he is a "royal" pain in the buttocks.

This kid has already been sent to Alternative School THREE TIMES!! Once as a first grader and twice as a second grader. Naturally, if he hopes to follow the established mathematical pattern, he's got to step it up in order to visit "baby jail" three times this year as a third grader. And he's already well on his way.

We are only midway through the first week of school, and Roy'al has already been suspended for the rest of the week.

You may be wondering, what could he possibly have done to warrant a suspension this soon?
Chewing gum in class?
Nah, too mundane.
Playing in the bathroom?
Not adventurous enough.
Running down the hall, wearing a cape and underwear outside his pants, screaming, "Look at me! I'm Master of the Marble Men!" while sprinkling fresh-grated parmesan everywhere?
Of course not – nobody does that!

No, Roy'al decided to cuss at a little girl in his class and then punch her in the stomach. Or maybe he punched her first and then dropped the F-bomb. Either way, it was two wrongs, which never make a right. However, two wrongs CAN lead to a suspension.

I feel bad for Mrs. Fitzgerald and Mrs. Frisch, who will have to deal with this kid all year. Still, I will gladly take an overload of students and push the boundaries of maximum kiddage rather than have Roy'al in my class. After all, if our skeleton project today is any indication, I already have enough kids trying to put their heads up their rear ends.
Later,

Pat Tella

Date: Friday, August 28, 2009
To: Fred Bommerson
From: Jack Woodson
Subject: Safety is job five

Hey Fred,

Wow, what a first week of school! They still haven't fixed the air conditioning in our wing, and I saw the classroom thermometer as high as 85° today after recess. The sweltering heat makes it nearly unbearable, but I guess I've never fully appreciated the HVAC's secondary function, which is to carry away undesirable odors. Without a working A/C, the classroom is RIPE with sweaty B.O. after recess!

To answer your question, yes, it's a huge difference between classes now because of the numbers. After my homeroom 21 (yep, got a new one) leave at 10:30 and Mrs. Bird's 14 come in, it feels like there are miles between populated desks. Of course you're right, it makes sense to move a few kids over to 3B and even out my classes, but we can't do that just yet. Every year we level things out after the first six weeks. By then, the numbers may very well have evened out a bit. At the very least, the kids should have a better grasp of their bone system by then.

Speaking of which, now you've got that song "Bad to the Bone" stuck in my head. Thanks a lot. Expect an a cappella version of "MMMBop" on your voicemail real soon.

No skeleton puzzles in class today; instead, my kids made science safety posters. Each group of two or three students had chosen a slogan such as "Always cover your clothes with an apron," or "Always wash your hands after an experiment." The posters were not exactly OSHA-quality, but they definitely provided some grins and giggles (griggles).

The early morning group who had chosen "Be careful around sharp objects" drew some very colorful pictures of kids having their eyes stabbed out, their hands cut off, and their backs punctured with forks.

Clear message? Check.

Another group, who had "Always wear safety goggles," drew a tiny figure with goggles atop an erupting volcano. If only the poor citizens of Pompeii had worn safety goggles.

I found myself almost wishing that the old lady from the district office would stop by again, like she did my first year, to proclaim, "I think safety goggles are SEXY!"

In the afternoon class, a couple of girls had written a very confusing slogan on their poster – "Mittens with hands always wear bad." They had drawn an equally confusing picture that seemed to show chemicals dripping on someone's hands, causing bloody stigmata to bloom.

Before you ask, these girls are NOT from Japan, so we can safely assume they had nothing to do with the instructions that come with every batch of solder at Heat Pumps – "Must do not lick up solder unsafe."

Later in the afternoon, we had a couple of incidents that flew in the face of those safety posters.

At recess, one of Mrs. Frisch's boys jumped out of a swing at its highest point. Displaying incredibly anti-feline tendencies, he did NOT land on his feet. Instead, he served as a cautionary tale in a new video safety series I'm creating called "The Playground Is Red."

In all seriousness, it was a relatively minor injury, and I think there was a much larger quantity of tears than blood that came out of the boy. The school nurse took a look at him and sent him back with a wet paper towel and a bandage on his noggin.

The other unsafe moment came at the end of the day, when I almost lost a student.

Because of the high temperatures and the lack of rain, a lot of the earth out by the buses has separated, creating narrow holes, some of which are about a foot deep. I was leading my kids out to the buses when I suddenly heard a yelp from behind me. I turned around and saw that one of Felipe's legs had disappeared up to the knee! He had stepped in one of the sinkholes and now looked upset, hurt, and confused all at once.

He's not a tall boy to begin with, and everyone standing around staring at him now appeared to be twice his size.

I hooked my hands under his armpits and lifted him out of the hole, but his shoe remained wedged in the earth! I had to get down on my hands and knees to reach down into the pit and work it free.

Thankfully, I got all of the kids to their buses without further incident. I've never lost a student in my teaching career, and I wasn't about to let some wannabe Sarlaac Pit ruin my track record in the first week of school!

Mrs. Frisch later commented ominously that she hopes the sinkhole will still be there when Roy'al returns from suspension. If it is, I may need to provide safety goggles to my students for that perilous trek out to the bus. Let's just hope there are no dormant volcanoes waiting to erupt.
Talk to you later,

Hole-ly Moses

Date: Tuesday, September 1, 2009
To: Fred Bommerson
From: Jack Woodson
Subject: Diarrhea of a wimpy kid

Hey Fred,

Either it's an incredibly eerie coincidence that your A/C is out at work too, or you should be very concerned that my school district has taken over HPU. Either way, it's going to get real hot, real soon, so I hope for both our sakes that the problem is fixed quickly.

By the way, your (far too vivid) description of a sweat-soaked Larry will give me nightmares for weeks to come.

I'll see what I can do about getting you a few of those safety posters to put up around the manufacturing floor. No doubt seeing those crayon-rendered depictions of tragedy will inspire the assemblers to follow their safety procedures more cautiously – AND make them fearful that management has lost their marbles.

I'm about to lose my own marbles here. Only seven days into the school year, and already I've received about 800 requests to go to the restroom. This is in addition to our regularly scheduled class bathroom breaks, mind you.

Breaks which usually take three times longer than they should, courtesy of the girls.

When we take our class breaks, I send four boys and four girls into their respective bathrooms. As each child comes out, another goes in, until everyone is finished. The entire group of boys is usually finished before the first girl has even exited. This is not the case with my afternoon class, which includes a couple of boys who sit in the bathroom for nearly ten minutes after lunch each day. I feel like I should start offering Tyler and Antonio a copy of the Wall Street Journal to peruse during their "thinking time."

Back to the morning class, though, and the girls. After a few bathroom breaks that seemed to last longer than The English Patient, I asked Miss Palmerstein, another third grade teacher, to stick her head in the girl's restroom and find out what was going on with my kids. She told me that she saw a girl walk into the bathroom, push open the first stall door, give a long, lingering look at whatever was inside, and then move to the next stall to repeat the process.

Now that I know what they're doing, when things seem to be moving slowly, I shout in at them, "Just pick one and go! Stop comparison shopping!"

We take our class break around 9:00 each morning. The kids know that. Still, it doesn't stop them from asking individually if they can make the trip, sometimes as early as 8:05!

Today, I finally decided to take a moment of class time and read to them "The Boy Who Cried Wolf." Primarily so that I could follow it up with my own version of the story – "The Kid Who Cried Bathroom."

It's usually fairly obvious when a child is truly having a potty emergency and when they are trying to fake it. Especially when they feel the need to accompany their request with an exaggerated version of the Pee Pee Dance, suggesting that if I don't immediately say yes, the room is going to be flooded.

However, I have had kids leak on themselves – remember "My bowels be runnin'" from long ago? – and that is never a good thing. So now I am always leery about what basically comes down to a game of "bathroom chicken."

Student X:	"I gotta use it!"
Me:	"We just took a class bathroom break twenty minutes ago."
Student X:	"It's an emergency!!"
Me:	"Come on, you just went. You don't need to go again."
Student X:	"Oh yeah? Watch this!"

[Student's face starts turning red, grunting sounds begin emanating, thin sheen of sweat appears on student's brow…]

In my never ending quest to prevent self-soilage AND deception, I have found two tricks that usually work pretty well. The first is to give the student a choice in the matter. "OK, you can go to the restroom now, but you'll have to sit out for five minutes of recess, OR, you can hold it."

I call that my "Sponge Statement," because it's amazing how often those words will seem to immediately soak up the impending deluge in the kid's bladder and allow him to resume his class work with ease.

The second trick, when I'm pretty sure that they really do need to go, is to time them. I usually give the boys one minute and the girls two minutes, and I tell them that if they're not sitting back at their desks again when that time is up, they will miss 10 minutes of recess (or 15, or 22 ½, or whatever strikes my fancy at the time).

Of course there are some kids who couldn't care less about whether they have recess or not. These are usually the same kids that consistently do not do their homework or bring back required signatures from their parents. But those kids are the exception, and those two tricks have worked pretty well for the majority of my kids.

For the others, I'm thinking about printing out a copy of "The Kid Who Cried Bathroom" for their lengthy stall visits. If they're going to miss math instruction, they may as well work on their reading skills.

Talk to you later,

Willie Makeit

Date: Friday, September 4, 2009
To: Fred Bommerson
From: Jack Woodson
Subject: Your answer doesn't make any cents

Hey buddy,

Though it might seem fun, I don't know that I'd suggest giving Larry a time constraint when he goes to the bathroom. Isn't he the one who boasts loudly about staying in there until his legs go numb? You may as well put a copy of War and Peace in there.

And leave it to Tom Winter to mix up his stories. The REAL story is "The Boy Who Cried Wolf." MY story is "The Kid Who Cried Bathroom." Tell Winter to stop crying "WOLF!" while IN the bathroom!

Enough potty humor. Let's move on to one of my favorite subjects – money, money, money!

Our topic for the week has been counting and adding money. The kids have to identify a collection of coins in a picture and then find the total amount of money.

I have bucketsful of fake money to use when I teach this topic. I've got plastic coins of all denominations and bright green paper bills. When I first pass these out and let the kids begin using them, I always make the announcement, "This is not real money! Please do not steal any of it from me and then try to go buy a Slurpee with it!"

Most of the kids laugh at my joke, but every year I hear a small, "Awwww!"

Today, we were going over the homework and I noticed that one of the problems had coins that were all showing a tail side. There was a quarter, a dime, and a couple of nickels. I pointed this out to the kids and advised them that they would need to be able to recognize the tail images as well as the heads to get money questions right. We agreed that the quarter has an image of an eagle, and the dime shows a picture of a torch. Then I asked what the image on the back of the nickel was. Most of the kids shouted out, "The White House!" but in my afternoon class, Mickey beat them all to the punch, shouting out, "That's the big jail house!"

Sadly, no. A nickel might be the hourly wage for someone living IN the big jail house, but it does not display such an image. And E Pluribus Unum is NOT Latin for, "Don't drop the soap."

Ella was having other money problems on Wednesday. I spent about ten minutes with her on what started out as a simple question.

She had written "200 cents" as an answer for one of her questions. I asked her, "What is another way we could say that?"

She stared at me uncomprehendingly, so I tried to clarify. I said, "That answer is not wrong, but usually when the number is that high, we use a different unit for money. Can you say 200 cents a different way, using that other unit?"

She thought for a moment and then responded, "200 dollars?"

Since cents and dollars are not the exact same thing, her response began the long, complicated discussion of how many cents are in one dollar. Getting that answer out of her was like pulling teeth. Teeth that apparently would have wildly fluctuating values for the tooth fairy.

I asked Ella to imagine that she had one dollar in her pocket, and I asked how many cents that would equal. She corrected me and informed me that she actually had SEVEN dollars in her pocket. My mistake.

I tried a different tact. I asked if she were to give me one of her dollars, how many cents would I need to give her for it to be a fair trade? One cent was her answer.

I immediately made the trade and moved on to the next student.

Just kidding. I continued my gluttony for punishment and jumped back into the conversation.

"So you could give me one dollar bill, and I could give you one penny, and that would be fair?" I asked.

Her head said no, but her eyes said she had no clue.

Ella's next guess was that one dollar was equal to twenty-five cents. So I took a quarter out of my pocket, placed it on her desk, and asked, "This equals one dollar?"

"Four cents?" was her reply.

Although she was grossly wrong, I thought I understood where that answer had come from and that it meant she was at least stumbling towards the right path. Sure enough, when pressed further, she confirmed that she had gotten that last answer by adding the quarter four times.

So I asked her to write down twenty-five cents four times on her paper and add them up. She did that and came up with – gasp – 100 cents.

"Yes, one dollar equals one hundred cents!" I confirmed. "So how many dollars would TWO hundred cents be worth?"

"Seven dollars?"

At that moment, I honestly felt like I was stuck in the middle of a MasterCard commercial.

"Math Journal – One dollar and fifty cents.
Demonstration Quarter – Twenty-five cents.
Incomprehensible Mathematics Conceptual Error – Seven dollars.
Bleeding head wound, caused by pounding my head on the surface of the desk – Priceless."

Talk to you later,

Seven Dollar Billy

Date: Tuesday, September 8, 2009
To: Fred Bommerson
From: Jack Woodson
Subject: I ain't got time to bleed

Hey dude,

Wow. Those guys at LaserTel sound like a bunch of winners. Bring them down to my classroom sometime and we can all conference together. That way, maybe Ella will finally learn what 200 cents is equal to, and the LaserTel guys will finally learn that 200 cents will only buy them about an eighth of a heat pump. Until then, it sounds like we both should buy stock in Motrin for banging our heads against solid objects.

Also, please tell Tom Winter that his suggestion of screaming, "SHOW ME THE MONEY!!" in Ella's face is not conducive to a learning environment.

Did I tell you that I have a hemophiliac in my class this year? No, that's not a girl with a Wee Willie Wahoo – that would be a hermaphrodite. Hemophilia is a condition where the blood doesn't clot properly.

It's actually a very big deal, because if Lance got cut, or even scratched, he might lose a lot of blood before it could be stopped. Accordingly, at the beginning of the year, Nurse McCaffrey brought a passel of paperwork around to all of Lance's teachers explaining the condition and making it clear that he was to be sent to the clinic immediately if anything ever happened.

You might think then that Lance would be a very methodical, reserved, careful child. You might also think that gold plated ceramics make a nice Mother's Day present. You would be wrong on both counts.

Lance is just as reckless and rambunctious as they come, and I'm amazed that I haven't had to send him to the nurse every day.

The lucky streak ended today, though. I was passing out a worksheet to all of the kids, when from behind me I heard someone cry out, "I'm bleeding!"

This proclamation was not shrieked in horror or screamed with any sense of pain or urgency. It was more in the tone of someone impatiently waiting to place a food order – "I'm ready now!"

My heart stopped for a second, and as I turned around in slow motion, I thought, "Please don't be him. Please don't be him."

Sure enough, it was Lance, looking down at a paper cut on his finger. A paper cut, that most minor and insignificant of scrapes. It's the Detroit Lions of bodily injuries.

Nevertheless, a paper cut could be disastrous for someone like Lance, so I flew into action. "Go to the clinic! Now! No, you don't need a nurse's slip or a hall pass! JUST. GO. NOW!"

I got him out the door in about five seconds. As I was walking back to the center of the room, Jessie, who also sits at Lance's table, said, "I think I have a paper cut, too."

"Oh, you'll be fine," I said, without even glancing at him.

That Teacher of the Year distinction will NOT elude me this year!

Switching from quick bleeders to slow thinkers, I encountered yet another concrete example of the lack of problem solving capabilities that I am facing this year. As we were switching classes, one of the girls in the afternoon group named Chassany came into my room bawling. I escorted her out into the hallway and away from the class to give her some room and some time to compose herself while the rest of the class got settled in and started on the word problem up on the board. Then I went back out to talk with her about what was going on.

Chassany told me that she was crying because she had gotten in trouble with Mrs. Bird for talking in the hall. I asked her, quite rationally I thought, what she could do to prevent that from happening again. She stared at me, dumbfounded.

I prompted her, "Do you have any ideas?"

She just gave me that miniscule shoulder shrug that seems to speak volumes. It conveys everything from, "I dunno," to, "Frankly, I don't care enough to even pretend that I'm interested in attempting to think of an answer to your question. Also, I have no idea what your question even was."

I spoke as slowly and as calmly as I could. "You got in trouble for talking in the hallway, right?" I asked her. When she nodded, I continued, "So what do you think you should do so that you DON'T get into trouble again?"

Nothing but a blank face. She had absolutely no answer for me. It's not like she was being sullen and refusing to speak. She really and truly didn't have any clue how she could avoid getting into trouble for talking in the hall.

Awesome.

Oh, and have I mentioned that Chassany is obsessed with my hair? Every time I talk to her, I can tell that her eyes are focused on the top of my head. She seems to have no interest in the buzz cuts, fauxhawks, and "booty fades" worn by her classmates, but for some reason my haircut fascinates her.

Today's conversation was no different. Even through all the tears, I could see her glancing up above my forehead.

I just wanted to shout, "Excuse me, young lady, my eyes are down here!"

I will admit that when my hair is cut short, like it is now, it can look a bit spiky in front. I suppose in addition to weathering Chassany's stares, I'll have to be on guard against scraping Lance with a sharp lock of hair.

That would not look good on a resume.

Talk to you later,

Flo B. Woodson

Hey buddy,

Like I said, I'm amazed that this was the first time I'd had to send Lance to the clinic. FYI, I'm pretty sure I can't just duct tape him to his seat to keep him out of harm's way, as you suggested. Not everybody appreciates the full spectrum of uses for duct tape.

You're right, Ron Philby would not qualify as a hemophiliac, but he definitely is a hair-o-philiac. And here I thought enough time had passed for people to forget that I didn't start using hair gel until I had been at Heat Pumps for a few years, and that my first couple of attempts were less than smooth. Please inform Latya that my student, Chassany, merely stares at my hair. She doesn't constantly point at it and shout, "There's something about Mary!" like HE did.

Today, I just wanted to pull all of my hair out. My kids this year seem exceptionally low. Maybe I'm practicing selective amnesia and choosing to forget that I ALWAYS have this opinion in September, but I don't think so. It feels awfully early for me to already be weighing the option of a career in online marketing.

I gave a math test today, and the subject was addition. There were several computation problems that allowed the kids to show (or disprove) their mastery of basic facts and regrouping (what we used to call carrying), a couple of word problems, and one short answer question.

There weren't many issues with the computation problems, as these were pretty simple, and most of the kids understand regrouping when it comes to addition. Several kids are still counting on their fingers, but at least they are coming up with the right answers. Even Priya, who goes out of her way to be a time sink in class – she once stopped the class after I wrote $15 + 7 = ?$ to ask, "What are those two lines?" – understands regrouping and even got both word problems correct. ("Those two lines" were the equal sign, by the way.)

The word problems were very basic, and it was obvious that the entire test was over the topic of addition. Still, that didn't stop Franco from subtracting on one of them, even though the question asked for a total. Two other students added numbers that weren't even in the problem. That's just sloppy.

Word problems, even simple ones, are always sticky with my kids because they either can't, won't, or don't want to read them carefully. However, reading looks like their strong suit when you compare it to their writing.

The last question on the test was free response, and it said, "What is the math word that means 'the answer to an addition problem?'"

Before the kids began the test, I talked about this question, hoping there wouldn't be so much confusion. I told them that I just wanted ONE WORD that is the special math name for the answer we get when we add. This is a word that we have spoken nearly every day in class.

Out of both classes combined, I had 15 kids that wrote the correct word, "sum."

Here are some of the wrong answers I received:

Add (so obvious, yet so wrong)
Math addition (as opposed to social studies addition?)
Altogether (a helpful clue word, but not the answer)
Forty thousand ninety three (only for a very specific addition problem)
OGO (guess who wrote THAT one!)
The plus sign (the ANSWER is not called the plus sign!!)
Mr. Woodson (kiss butt much?)
Shug you whorek (at first, I thought I had been insulted in Klingon, but then I realized Joaqim meant "show your work")

Really, this is just laziness. As far as vocabulary words go, "sum" is certainly one of the easier ones. I can't wait until we get into the subtraction words. Subtrahend and minuend – those sound like words straight out of a horror movie.

On an unrelated note, I just saw that I could be making $12,000 a month selling real estate from the comfort of my office chair. It's something to consider.

Talk to you later,

Add 'em Ant

Date: Monday, September 14, 2009
To: Fred Bommerson
From: Jack Woodson
Subject: Identity Crisis

Hey bud,

That's right, I called Priya a time sink. Heat sinks, which we are intimately familiar with, draw away heat from a source. Time sinks, like certain children I know, draw away valuable minutes from a lesson, dispersing them to the four winds, never to be reclaimed again. My time sinks are highly efficient, too!

Once again, it's Monday, and as some people my parents' age once sang – Monday, Monday, can't trust that day. As opposed to Friday, which I would trust with my life, my banking password, and my vintage Star Wars action figure collection.

Still, the Mondays of this year, as well as most every day, have been made brighter by a certain ray of sunshine in my class. Her name is Katie, and she always seems to have a smile on her face. There have been several mornings when I have been ticked off well before 8:15 am – kids not having their homework, kids somehow needing to trade pencils ten times in ten minutes, kids insisting a triangle has four sides – and when I've walked around the room like a sourpuss. On these occasions, Katie always has a way of looking up from her morning work, catching my eye, flashing her brilliant smile, and then going right back to work.

After that, there's just no way I can remain angry. At least not until Lakeisha opens her mouth again.

If Katie is the ray of sunshine, then the new kid I got today is the flashlight beam through murky water.

Ever since school started, I've been hearing about this new kid that I was supposed to get named Kevin. He's a special ed kid, so Ms. Hamm and Miss Knox have been coordinating things and heralding his arrival.

First, it was, "Kev will be here on Thursday." Then, "Kevin will be here next Tuesday." Finally, "We're really not sure why Kev isn't here yet."

At long last, Kevin showed up today. I saw the new kid in my line this morning, and I greeted him warmly with the name I had heard most often. "Hi! You must be Kev!"

DaQuayvius immediately corrected me – "It's Kevin!"

I sometimes think DaQuayvius must have thirty fingers, because he seems to have a finger in everyone's business. I have no doubt he knows Kevin's entire life story after spending a mere twenty minutes with him in the gym.

I gave DaQuayvius a quick stink eye then asked the new boy, "What do you prefer to be called, Kevin or Kev?"

He mulled it over then answered, "Well, sometimes people call me Kevin, and some people call me Kev. But my real name is Anferny. My mom just likes how Kevin sounds."

Not once had I heard the name "Anferny" mentioned in any discussions about this kid, so I had my suspicions. I asked him, "So what should I call you – Kevin or Kev?"

He replied, "Anferny."

OK, we have a winner. For the next thirty minutes, I called him Anferny. "Anferny, do you have a pencil?" "Anferny, come and get a math journal." "Did you learn how many cents are in a dollar at your old school, Anferny?"

At about half past eight, Miss Knox dropped by to see how the new kid was doing. When I told her about the name change, her mouth dropped, and she took "Anferny" out into the hallway to speak with him. A couple of minutes later, they came back into my classroom, and the little boy said to me with a sheepish grin, "You can call me Kev now."

Oooooookay...

If this happens again tomorrow, I'm going to make an executive decision and start calling him Doofenshmirtz.

After helping "Kev" with his identity crisis this morning, it seemed a little anti-climactic that our after school staff meeting would be all about the Campus Crisis Plan. Back in mid-August, we were each given a document roughly the size of the Greater Chicago Area phone directory and told to memorize it. This document was the Crisis Plan, and in brief, it tells us what to do in the case that a crazed gunman or bomb-toting maniac wanders into our school. Basically, we lock the doors, pull the blinds, and cower beneath our desks. Oh, and we are also supposed to slide a special green laminated card under our door into the hallway, telling everyone that we are A-OK.

Not surprisingly, many of us were wondering just who was going to see that sign, if we were all locked in our rooms. Are we putting out the sign for the benefit of the maniac stalking the halls? If so, should it really be the green sign, or the red "All is NOT OK" card? Or do we slide out the green one, and then once the maniac starts trying to break down our door, slide out the red one – real subtle-like?

In order to test our new knowledge, we played a mock version of Jeopardy. Hopefully, I am not the only one who saw the irony in this.

Not that it's a bad idea to have a crisis plan on hand. It might have been nice to have one at HPU that time the guy crashed his cocaine-laden SUV into the corner of our offices and then ran off into the sand pit next door. Though it was exciting for all of us to stand around on the delivery dock in back watching the police search the area with dogs and helicopters, I think that if there had been a crisis plan in place, you never would have dared me to rip my shirt off and run wildly across the parking lot. Of course, if I had taken your dare, I doubt I would be here writing you this email right now.

I might instead be trying to convince some scary person that my name really is Anferny as I subtly slide a red laminated card under the door.

See ya later,

Dan Jerzone

Date: Wednesday, September 16, 2009
To: Fred Bommerson
From: Jack Woodson
Subject: Clothing arguments

Hey man,

Absolutely, I hope and pray that nothing of the sort ever happens here at my school. But there are whackjobs all around us, and it doesn't hurt to be aware of such things. Just to clarify, though, the crisis plan is meant to deal with major incidents at the school. Antonio disappearing in the bathroom for half an hour, while challenging, doesn't really qualify as a crisis.

A different type of problem is the clothing crisis I see going on around me. I had to ask Mrs. Fitzgerald today why she clearly has not yet had a discussion with her students about acceptable and unacceptable attire. One of her kids was wearing a sweatshirt today, and what bothered me wasn't just the fact that he was wearing it outside, even though the temperature hasn't dipped below 95 degrees yet. By now, I'm used to seeing kids run around the playground on a 100 degree day bundled up like they're shoplifting from Burlington Coat Factory.

What irritated me was that this was a University of North Carolina sweatshirt.

I've never really understood why UNC gear is so universally popular. Maybe it's because Michael Jordan went there? Or Vince Carter for the younger generation? I'm guessing it's not for love of Ed Cota or Serge Zwikker. But whatever the reason, I used to see kids wearing UNC's baby blue all the time before the district implemented a dress code.

Whenever I saw a child wearing UNC apparel, I said a silent prayer for the child's soul, but I generally let it go at that. I don't want to scar any kids' psyches after all. I remember all too well a disturbing incident from when I was a child myself.

I'm originally from the Washington, DC area, and I was raised as a Redskins fan. When I was around seven years old, I was at a bowling alley here in Texas with my parents, proudly wearing my burgundy Redskins jacket. I remember this big guy, obviously a Cowboys fan, walking by and saying, "Hey kid! Com'ere and gimme that jacket so I can flush it down the toilet!"

If I had been five or six years older, I might have pointed out to him the finer points of fluid dynamics and plumbing, in order to make him aware that his proposed action was not completely practical. However, as a seven-year-old, I was too concerned with his size, the inherent threat of his slurred statement, and the odd aroma of old bread and raisins arising from his personage.

I'm not ever going to threaten to flush a kid's sweatshirt. But I AM glad that I'm tempted far less often since the dress code was implemented this year. All elementary students now wear a white collared shirt and navy or tan slacks, shorts, or skirt. The white shirt looks nice in the morning but then winds up looking like a Twister mat after lunch, with Hot Cheeto stains, fruit juice spills, and nacho cheese flavor pockets.

At first, I didn't really think a dress code was necessary. It's certainly possible that having to wear identical outfits has narrowed the gap between the haves and the have-nots, but probably not, since there really aren't many haves at my school. I don't remember anyone flaunting their Versace, their Dolce and Gabbana, or even their LeTigre in the past.

I don't recall any insults or arguments relating to clothing back then, either. I would have remembered hearing a child taunt a classmate with, "Ha! Your T-shirt is an unflattering shade of red!"

Maybe the problem was more rampant at other schools throughout the district, and that's what necessitated the change.

Kids can still find ways to insult each other even within the confines of a dress code, though. When I was in elementary school, we had a uniform, and even though we were all wearing basically the same thing, I guess my pants were a little too short. The other kids called them "high waters." I can still remember classmates pointing at me and jeering, "You expecting a flood?"

I should have just waited until I saw one of those kids wearing a T-shirt in February and retorted, "Oh yeah? You expecting unseasonably warm temperatures before Spring?"

Again, I'm not aware of these specific problems at my school. I will say, though, one great thing about having a dress code is that I don't have to worry about my students coming in wearing sweatpants with the word, "Juicy" stitched across their rear end.

I never understood why any parent would let their child go to school wearing something like that (why not save it for Grandma's 80th birthday party?), but then I'm amazed by a lot that kids encounter at home, including their own parents' personal dress code.

Miss Rooker, our school counselor, told me a story several years ago about a visit she made to a student's home. The mother of the student answered the door wearing a T-shirt and flip-flops – and nothing else. The woman was not wearing anything from the waist down!

I told Miss Rooker that would have been the perfect time to use the phrase, "I find your lack of pants disturbing."

But I ask you, how can a child NOT be majorly screwed up when there is such blatant "Porky Pigging" going on at home?

Having a dress code does create a brand new set of rules to enforce. Occasionally, kids have been sent home for being out of uniform, but that usually only happens if the principal spots it. Every once in a while, one of my kids will show up in a white T-shirt or non-regulation pants, but I'm not planning on sending any-one home for it. I've heard priests say that they're not going to dismiss anyone from Mass for their clothing because they would rather have them there at church, regardless of wardrobe. I feel the same way about the kids and school. With a few notable excep-tions, I'd rather have them in class than make them miss a day just because of their outfit.

My biggest challenge now is the rule that all students must have their shirts tucked in. Most kids think that a tucked-in shirt makes them look dorky, while I happen to feel that a kid wearing a shirt that goes down to his knees looks like he should be carrying a cleaver and a freshly cut slab of beef.

Quite often, when I ask a child to tuck his shirt in, he only tucks it in in the front, leaving the back and sides hanging out. THAT doesn't look dorky?

The Battle of the Tuck is an uphill struggle because some-how these shirts always manage to untuck themselves about five minutes after being tucked in. Last week, I made up a couple of names to go with the shirt status. A kid with his shirttail out is now "Slobby McSlopslop," while one with his shirttail in is "Spiffy McNeato." I can go down the line in my class and say, "Hi, Spif-fy!" or, "Hey, Slobby!" and the kids know exactly what I'm talking about.

Truth be told, I can't say that this has caused the kids to tuck in their shirts any more than they did before. But it does add a little humor to the situation, and the children laugh as they tuck their shirts in (and then untuck them as soon as my back is turned). Now I just have to deal with the Talky McBlabbermouths, the Snitchy McTattletales, and the Burpy McFlatulents.
Later,

The Shirttail Vigilante

Hey bud,

I really don't see how you can say you don't understand my gag-factor with Carolina blue. You know how Carol's cubicle is all decorated in Aggie swag (Swaggie?), and how she always wears maroon tops? You know how that always annoys you because you don't like A&M? Yeah, that's it exactly.

Oh, and if you could get a picture of Larry wearing "Juicy" sweatpants, I would pay good money for that. The Photoshop possibilities are virtually limitless.

This morning, I was checking the backs of the kids' homeworks to make sure they had shown their work. We've been doing place value charts – ones, tens, hundreds – for every problem. Most of the kids had done this as they were supposed to. "Most" unfortunately would not include Franco.

Glancing at the back of his paper, I saw no work whatsoever. Before I could even ask him where his place value charts were, he excitedly pronounced, "I did it a different way!"

He was really proud of himself, too, as if he had just discovered particle theory on his own.

I might not have been as gentle as I could have been when I pointed out to him that merely filling in an answer bubble was not really considered a "way," per se.

I did teach the kids "the way" to do a science experiment this week. We did a project called the Bubble Gum Lab, and we finished it today. In addition to the fact that it was listed on our curriculum planning guide, I thought it was important to conduct this experiment because of this question that popped up on last year's science benchmark test:

"Mrs. Cassidy's class was conducting a bubble gum experiment. They wanted to see what would happen to the mass of a piece of bubble gum when it is chewed. What is the best hypothesis for this experiment?

A) the mass of the bubble gum will increase.

B) the mass of the bubble gum will decrease.

C) the mass of the bubble gum will stay the same.

D) the mass of the bubble gum will change color."

I might not have gotten the wording of the question exactly right, but it did basically boil down to, "Which of these is the best hypothesis?"

Now, help me out here, buddy – check my science – but I'm pretty sure that when it comes to hypotheses, there are no better or worse. A hypothesis is merely a prediction that you hope to prove or disprove over the course of your experiment. If you already knew what was going to happen, you wouldn't be making a hypothesis – you would be stating a conclusion or a fact.

For example, "Five kids will ask to use the restroom within the next 20 minutes" – hypothesis.

"Chicks dig calculator watches" – fact.

So tell me if you disagree, but it seems to me that this is a horrendous question. Since I am merely a commonplace third grade teacher (i.e., lowly peon), no one who actually writes these tests listens or responds when I bring this up.

Therefore, I decided that my kids should definitely have the experience and know the conclusion, just in case this awful question rears its head once again on this year's benchmark. Teaching to the test? Absolutely guilty. At least the kids got some hands-on experience, though.

Yesterday, we wrote out all of the introductory sections – Problem, Hypothesis, Materials, and Procedure. The hypothesis was, "I think that the mass of the bubble gum will _____ when it is chewed." I wrote the four choices on the board and let each kid fill in the blank with his or her own opinion.

Thankfully, no one chose "change color." When I took a quick poll in each class, the other three options all had takers, and there was no overwhelming favorite.

Today, we carried out the experiment. I'm sure that the intention of the original writers of this lab was to have each individual child weigh their unchewed piece of gum, then again weigh their piece of gum after each minute of chewing. I calculated that if we did it that way, it would take us roughly 217,089 minutes of class time. Figuring we didn't really have that much time, I decided that all of the kids would be able to do the chewing part, but that everyone could watch as I weighed MY piece of gum each time.

When I pulled the packs of Orbitz gum out of my desk and started to unwrap them, several kids called out, "What flavor did you get?"

I replied, "Lemon-lime," and suddenly there was a unified chorus of gasps and cheers.

You would have thought that I had just parachuted out of a helicopter and into the classroom, holding a ginourmous bag of cash in one hand and a dragon's egg in the other.

I had somebody pass out a piece of gum to everyone while I set up the balance on a table in the front of the classroom. The first step of our procedure was to unwrap the piece of gum, so we all did that, and no less than eight kids in each class held the wrapper up to their noses, inhaled deeply, and then shuddered with satisfaction. I know it sounds vulgar, but it really did remind me of Booger from Revenge of the Nerds, sniffing a pair of unmentionables after the panty raid on the girls' dormitory.

Moving on from that disturbing image, the kids held onto their gum while I weighed my piece on the balance in front of them. I called out the measurement, and everybody wrote the number down in the Results table in their science journals. Then we started chewing. We used the red second hand on the wall clock to chew for exactly one minute. At the end of one minute, everyone took the piece back out of their mouth, and the kids held their own pieces of gum while I weighed mine.

During this time, many of the kids commented on the flavor of the gum. There was one or two comments along the lines of, "Thanks, Mr. Woodson – this gum tastes great!" But most of the comments were more like, "This tastes SOOOOOOO good!" – spoken in a tone of voice that I would more commonly relate to a nicotine addict who, having involuntarily gone an entire weekend without access to his smokes, has just taken his first drag.

After the first minute, we chewed for another minute and weighed again. Chew, weigh, record. Chew, weigh, record. Lather, rinse, repeat. We did this until we had officially chewed the gum for five minutes. At the end of it all, the results were clear-cut. The mass of the gum had decreased by about half of its original mass.

This lead to cheers and taunting from the kids who had chosen that as their hypothesis. Meanwhile, the kids who had chosen another option either cried or secretly changed their journal entry so they could join in the cheering.

With my morning class, I let the kids continue to chew their gum until it was time to switch to Mrs. Bird's class. Then I held the trash can for them to spit out their gum as they filed past me out the door. However, my afternoon class finished the experiment at about

2:55, so there was a mad rush to get everything ready to go home, and I forgot to have them spit out their gum before they left.

As we were walking down the hall to go outside, Coach Keys, our PE teacher, noticed and asked one of the kids, "So they're letting you chew gum now?"

I heard him and replied, "Yeah, it's for science."

As if that was the world's greatest blanket explanation for everything.

If my kids picked up on that, I can imagine hearing about this conversation next week:

Teacher: "Did you just spit water on him and throw his pudding across the room?"
Student X: "Yeah, it's for science."
Teacher: "Oh, OK then. Carry on."

Have a great weekend, man. Do a little science. Chew a little gum. Get down tonight. Get down tonight.
Have a good one,

Forest Gum

Date: Tuesday, September 22, 2009
To: Fred Bommerson
From: Jack Woodson
Subject: New Kids on the Clock

Hey Fred,

I would not recommend using the "It's for science" argument to explain a poor heat pump design at a production meeting. Paul and Reggie are both way more "science" than you or I could ever hope to be, so that phrase might come across as something close to blasphemy.

Thanks for telling me that Steve Potts is having surgery tomorrow. I'll be sure to keep my old boss in my prayers. If you see him today, tell him it's okay to have his appendix removed, and maybe even his index, but nobody better lay a hand on his glossary.

Now that a few weeks have passed, I've had more of a chance to get to know my kids and their quirks.

There's a boy named Eddie in my morning class that I may as well call Simon. This is because if I ever want him to do anything, I have to actually address him by name. If I don't, it's like he doesn't even hear me.

So I find myself forced to play Simon Says. If I say to the class, "Boys and girls, please take out your science books," then nearly everyone will take out their science books, EXCEPT for Eddie. He'll just sit there at his desk, totally oblivious to the actions going on around him.

However, if I say, "Eddie, please take out your science book," THEN he'll immediately do as he's asked.

He's very consistent about this. It's not a once or twice occurrence. So I've started making requests in the following manner.

"Eddie, and everyone else, please take out your science books."
"Eddie, and boys and girls, please stop writing, and take out something to grade with."
"Be sure to tuck your shirt in all the way around, Eddie – and everyone else."

Another little boy, Amir, is very friendly and intelligent, but he has some pretty odd characteristics. For one thing, he doesn't like to touch paper. I'm not just saying this as something I've observed. Amir actually told me that he can't stand the way paper feels, and it makes him want to throw up sometimes.

Remind me to look into printing up my homework on lambskin.

Amir works around this obstacle pretty well. He WILL occasionally touch paper (and really, in this environment, how could he not?), but for the most part, he uses a couple of pencils like tweezers or chopsticks to move the paper where he wants it on his desk. Then as he's writing, he doesn't touch that paper again. It's oddly fascinating to watch, but it explains why I can barely read what he writes.

Oh, and did I mention that he also carries a wet stick in his backpack?

Franco, the discoverer of a DIFFERENT way to do his homework (one that involved no work whatsoever), has another quirk. When called upon, he begins many of his answers with a chipmunk-quick, "Oh yeah, what's it called?" Just today, I asked him if 37 was odd or even. "Odd!" he shouted.

"Why is it odd?" I persisted.

"Oh yeah, what's it called, cuz the 7 doesn't have a partner?"

Then there's Big Jack. He and I share a name and a gender, but not much else. He lives up to his nickname in that he's about 4'10", which is big for a third grader. Also, he weighs around 150 lbs.

Big Jack has some Big ADHD. He is distracted by the merest thing, sometimes just the twitching of an ant's legs in the front office. To him, pencils are rocket ships, meant to blast off (loudly) and fly around and often crash into each other. I wouldn't be surprised to discover that he drinks three Red Bulls for breakfast every day, because he fidgets non-stop, and he throws out rapid-fire questions. He's always asking me if I like to perform various actions.

"Mr. Woodson, do you like to go bowling?"
"Mr. Woodson, do you like to go swimming?"
"Mr. Woodson, do you like to go Porky Pigging?"

I wouldn't mind so much, if he didn't ask these questions in the middle of class. I usually just respond, "I really like teaching and being listened to."

Also, I can expect to be asked, "Did I do good?" at least once a day from Big Jack. It doesn't matter whether he buckled down and focused (as much as he's able) or whether he floated breezily through Shiny Object Land, he never leaves without asking, "Mr. Woodson, did I do good today?"

I visited Mrs. Bird's room this morning to ask her something, and Big Jack had just contributed a verb to the list on the board. As he walked back to his seat, I was not at all surprised to hear him ask, "Did I do good, Mrs. Bird?"

I was tempted to say, "Eddie – and everyone else – please tell Big Jack that he did good."

Later,

Joe Kerse

Date:	Friday, September 25, 2009
To:	Fred Bommerson
From:	Jack Woodson
Subject:	Wine us, dine us, learn to minus

Hey bud,

How did I know that it would be Nancy who asked about the stick? Her skills as a customer service representative demand that she gets all the details.

I certainly can't explain WHY Amir carries a wet stick in his backpack, or even why it has to be wet. I can only tell you that it is about ten inches long, with a fork at one end. Maybe it's a dowsing rod, in case he needs to find the nearest water fountain? His mother advised me not to ask him about it when she dropped him off one morning. As long as it stays in the backpack, I'm honoring her request.

I think it's hilarious that you and Tiffany are going to start asking Larry, "Did I do good?" every time you give him a project update. I totally support that. Be sure to ignore him every time he doesn't address you by name as well.

It's nice that you're having fun at work, but once again, I am feeling majorly frustrated with these kids. There are a few very enthusiastic kids in my class, like Jessie and Jacob, but overall, the kids are really low, and they don't seem to care about improving that condition.

I've always understood (while simultaneously despising the fact) that a kid's brain over summer vacation is like a beach ball with a slow leak. They always come back acting like they've never heard of concepts like symmetry and perimeter. But what frustrates me most about this year is that my kids don't even know their basic facts. When most of the class needs to stop and count on their fingers for a question like "10 minus 9," I start to get worried!

Still, I prefer the counting on fingers to the random guessing. The kids this year are low on knowledge but high on competitiveness, and in their minds, being first completely outweighs being right.

For instance, last Wednesday in my afternoon class, I asked, "What is 8 minus 6?"

There was a low collective, "ummmmmmmmmmm" for about a second, and then the wild guessing began.

"SIX!"

"THREE!"

"EIGHT!"

"GREEN!"

OK, so no one said, "green." Thankfully. And Tyler DID shout out the right answer amidst all the others. But this was not a difficult question!

Regrouping, or borrowing, on the other hand is not an issue for them – since most of them don't do it!

"What is 12 minus 8?" I ask.

"SIXTEEN!!" the kids shout, as the high fives begin and the party favors get passed out.

Never mind that this is a totally unreasonable answer, since 16 is larger than the number they started with. 104 minus 98 apparently equals 194, 23 minus 7 is 24, and 200 minus 89 is, naturally, 289.

Even a lot of the high kids missed the problems that required borrowing on the pre-test I gave Monday. This is something they should have mastered in second grade, and it should be a quick review this year. Instead, I find myself having to teach it from scratch.

My Sir Mixalot approach to subtraction – "I like Big Bottoms with a Tiny Top!" – which worked fantastically last year, just has not stuck with the kids this year.

Recently, a teacher at another school passed on a little rhyme to me, so I've been giving that a try. It's a mantra that goes, "If there's more on the top, no need to stop. If there's more on the floor, let's go next door and get ten more. If the numbers are the same, then zero is the game."

I thought it was super cheesy when I first heard it, but when I recited it in front of the class on Tuesday, the kids loved it! It really seems to be sticking, too, because more of them are remembering more frequently to regroup. Getting them to actually recite the rhyme has been a little bit more of a challenge, though. When I try to get them to explain why they need to regroup, I've heard a few mishmashes like, "If there's more on the bottom, let's go next door. And get another ten!"

I should make a note to ask Mrs. Bird to work on what makes a rhyme.

Still, they are slowly beginning to get the concept, and that is making a world of difference. Now if I could just get them to learn the WORD difference.

Remember that free response question on the addition test? Since it went over so well then, coupled with the fact that I'm a glutton for punishment, I put a similar question on today's test. "What is the math word that means, 'the answer to a subtraction problem?'"

Thirteen kids wrote, "Sum."

I think I would have been happier if they had written "GREEN." Culinary school is starting to look better and better. Just saying.

Talk to you later,

Tay Quay

Hey Fred,

Tom Winter sent me a note on Monday with a slightly modified version of my subtraction rhyme. I'm not sure if he's shared it with you yet, so here it is:

"He's got more on the top, so his gut will flop. If he's down on the floor, he'll continue to snore, and get mocked some more. If zero is his game, then Bommerson is the name."

I'm thinking this will look lovely on an embroidered pillow in the corner of your cubicle.

I have to tell you, you read my mind, man. I would love to be able to model subtraction in the real world by subtracting a couple of kids from my class! Or let me at least send them to the doctor to treat that really nasty minus infection. As it is, I might have to settle for demonstrating subtraction by disallowing Hot Cheetos from the kids' diets and watching their weight go down.

I say this with one notable exception, because I think I have finally struck upon some true motivation for one of my really challenging kids!

Antonio is chubby, academically low, a talker, a player, a does-not-pay-attentioner, and generally an all-around "slug." On the first math test, this kid got a 25. On the second math test, he got a 17. These were not at all hard or unfair math tests, either. He just wasn't trying at all, and it showed.

Conversely, some of my other kids HAVE been picking it up quite a bit and trying harder. I am finally starting to get through to them that paying attention and doing their work the way we practice in class really CAN help them get the right answers and better grades.

In my homeroom, nearly every single one of my kids who had scored low on the first big test dramatically improved their grades on the second one, and the kids who had done well on the first test also did well on the second. One exception to this was Suzie, who seems to feel that math and science are not nearly as important as frequent napping. She's putting all of her chips on osmosis through her textbook/pillow, and it just hasn't paid off yet.

In my afternoon class, which contains Antonio the slug (and several other garden-variety slimers), I haven't seen quite the same dramatic results, but there were a few kids who improved and several who did pass both tests.

I decided to make a really big deal about this and highlight the kids who have been showing effort. At the very beginning of the year, I had gotten stacks of cards from Denny's, Golden Corral, and Popeye's which said, "Buy one adult meal, get one kid's meal free." I took the time to fill them out with the kids' names, my name, our school name, etc, along with the phrase "Math Improvement!" if they had bettered their score the second time around, or "Awesome Math Skills!" if they had passed both tests.

I gave these cards out on Monday. Everybody in my homeroom who got one loved it. Nestor saw the picture on one card and blurted out, "I LOVE the chicken of church!!"

"Um, do you mean Church's Chicken?" I asked.

"YEAH!" he shouted.

Somewhere around 60% of the students in my second class got a card, as there are still several kids with very poor grades. Obviously, Antonio was in the 40% who did NOT receive this reward.

This apparently struck a nerve. Or a salivary gland. On Tuesday, my "slug" started paying attention. He raised his hand to answer questions – and he answered them correctly! He brought his homework on Wednesday with work shown and completed. It was like a completely different kid had inhabited Antonio's body.

The kids took the 6-weeks cumulative assessment today, and Antonio, while not having everything correct, had work shown for every question. He had labeled his coins, he had drawn place value charts, and he had shown his addition and subtraction steps. When I graded the tests, I found that this "slug" – 25 on the first test, 17 on the second – had scored an 80 on the 6-weeks test. An EIGHTY!!

Maybe the planets aligned just right for him to finally get with the program. Maybe something I said about effort finally seeped through. Maybe he had all of the answers to the test written on the back of his fake eye patch.

But I have a feeling it was the idea of free food that finally jump-started his engine.

And you know what? I'm ok with that. I see nothing wrong with the old carrot and stick strategy, and if the carrot comes with a deep fried all you can eat buffet, all the better!

Somebody will most definitely be getting a Golden Corral coupon Monday afternoon.

My own fondness for fast food produced interesting ramifications today after recess. The girls in line were giggling and looking at me, so I asked what they were talking about. Tiny Anna spoke up and said, "I saw you and Mrs. Fitzgerald at Taco Bell."

The little girls around her giggled scandalously, and Big Jack, eyes wide as platters, demanded, "REALLY? You really saw them?"

We had in fact seen Tiny Anna and her family at the nearby Taco Bell back in August, the week before school started, during one of our teacher prep days. Why she had waited an entire grading period to bring this up is beyond me. Why this would be so scintillating to the other kids is beyond me. Why Big Jack would practically wet himself over this news is beyond me. However, I feel like I've learned a valuable lesson from this. Please be sure to remind me, if I ever decide to attempt an affair with a married coworker, to be sure NOT to take her to the local taco joint.

That is, unless I have a valid Buy One, Get One Free card to burn.

Talk to you later,

Cyrano de Burrito

Date: Monday, October 5, 2009
To: Fred Bommerson
From: Jack Woodson
Subject: You'll have to speak up, I'm wearing a tie

Hey Fred,

So what did Paul say when you proposed the idea of meal coupons for improved performance? (Not that I believe you really proposed it.) Were you aware that Larry has been known to use those "Buy one adult meal, get one child's meal free" coupons? It must be very off-putting for bystanders when the cashier says, "But sir, where is your child?" and Larry replies, "This card doesn't say I have to have a kid with me! Gimme my meals!"

I think my instinct was dead-on, by the way. When I presented Antonio with his free food card today, he lit up like a Christmas tree. You'd have thought that I had just offered him a starring role in "High School Musical 6: Get a GED Already!"

You do make a very valid point, though. If his slug side starts to return, I may very well need to offer TWO cards as an incentive next time around.

Last Thursday marked the end of the first six-weeks grading period. Friday was Fair Day – The State Fair, not "play impartially without cheating" – so there was no school. I spent my long weekend getting grades together and putting them into the computer. I've decided that preparing report cards would be a lot more fun if Nintendo would hurry up and develop Gradebook Hero for the Playstation or Wii.

Today is the first Monday of October, and that means a big change in how I come to work. The summer dress code is officially over. Never mind the fact that it's still over 100 degrees outside and even inside the classroom, I feel like a microwaved poodle. The HVAC units in our classrooms seem to have been cobbled together by drunk baby pandas in the 1950s, and they are just as likely to HEAT an already hot classroom as they are to cool it.

Nevertheless, now that it's October, I'm required to wear a tie and a button-down shirt. For me, this automatically means a long-sleeve shirt, because I just can't bring myself to wear a short-sleeve shirt with a tie and look like I stepped out of the NASA Apollo program of the '60s.

Our art teacher, Mr. Vann, decided a few years ago that he didn't like his tie hanging down into the clay/paint/whatever, so he started wearing a bow tie. This hasn't been challenged, so I'm thinking maybe I could start wearing a bolo and get away with it.

Or I could take a page from my old high school basketball coach, whom we called "The Guam Bomb." Every game day, our coach showed up wearing a Hawaiian shirt, a tie, sweat pants, and cowboy boots. The tie was always undone and hanging loosely by the time the game actually started.

Usually, the transition from casual to dressy goes unnoticed, or at least uncommented on, by my students. This year, though, I received several compliments.

"Nice tie!"
"You look great today!"
"I like your shirt!"
"Handsome!"
"You look like a businessman!"
"Is that 10 pounds of crap in a 5 pound bag?"

Just so you know, I threw that last one in as an example of the kind of thing that was NOT said to me today. Everything was very positive!

While my attire was new, the kids' level of confusion retained its status quo, as evidenced by a few things I heard today.

Mrs. Bird shared a funny story at lunch. She's been fed up with the rote, wooden, zombie-like nature of the kids' Pledge of Allegiance recital in the mornings, so she had them write out the Pledge on paper. In addition to a plethora of misspellings, one thing really stood out to her.

Victor had written (and I assume has been saying), "One Asian, under God..."

He must have forgotten where he lives, though he wasn't the only one geographically confused today. On our walk out to the buses, Isabel told me that when her dad gets out of jail (!), they are going to move away from the United States. I figured she meant they were moving to Mexico, so I jokingly asked her, "Oh, so you'll move to Japan?"

"No!" she answered.

"The moon?" I asked.

"No!"

When I asked her where they were going to move to, she replied, "To Miami."

Isabel's understanding of the world was less than ideal, and I suppose that could have been a carry-over from today's math lesson. We compared numbers in class, using the symbols for greater than, less than, and equal to. My kids seemed to grasp that concept pretty well for the most part. Of course, they really sank their teeth into the whole "alligator mouth eats the greater number" mnemonic. Literally. Almost all of them drew the symbols with jagged teeth, forked tongues, and in Jessie's case, fiery breath.

Mrs. Fitzgerald told me at lunch that one of the kids in her class looked at a problem where the two numbers were equal and declared, "The alligator don't know which side to eat!"

Unlike that alligator, I DO know which side to eat, and I'm hungry, so I'll let you go here. I've got a certain fast food card with my name on it, now all I need to do is find a kid to be my accomplice.

Talk to you later,

Ernie Quality

Date: Thursday, October 8, 2010
To: Fred Bommerson
From: Jack Woodson
Subject: Nobody likes a bad BM

What's up, Fred?

I will give you credit for being innovative and thinking of a creative "solution" to the shirt and tie issue. I will not be USING your solution, however. While I really like the idea of cutting a hockey score out of the newspaper – Stars 1, Avalanche 1 – and clipping it to my shirt, I don't think my principal would view it as a valid loophole.

Hey, you know that old theoretical exercise of putting a million monkeys at a million typewriters and seeing what they randomly produce? The old adage goes that eventually they would produce Hamlet and all of Shakespeare's other works of genius.

I'm not so sure about that, but I know what they COULD produce pretty quickly – the district Benchmark Tests!

We have to administer the Benchmark tests – or as I call them, BMs – twice every year. These things are horrible. They are poorly written, they have some super difficult questions on them, and they often don't even cover the topics we've been teaching.

The only good thing about BM days is that with half the day devoted to testing, my actual teaching periods are shortened, so the kids can't waste as much time.

The higher powers defend these tests by saying that the Benchmarks are harder than the TAKS, so the kids will do much better on the TAKS. This is like saying that running away from bulls in Pamplona is much harder than roller skating at the local Big Wheel.

This is the first set of standardized tests of the year, so it serves as TAKS practice for the kids. It also serves as practice for the teachers in monitoring random kids. For the past few years, we haven't been allowed to monitor our own kids during the TAKS. This is because of some educators south of here who cheated and helped their kids on the test. Now we all have to swap with teachers from other grade levels to ensure that we do not succumb to our base instinct for treachery and dishonesty. So on the TAKS days, my kids will take the test under the watchful eye of a teacher they may occasionally see in the hallway but whom they probably do not know very well. How does this affect their mood, temperament, anxiety level, and/or performance that day, you might ask? Well, imagine that the next time you drop your pants at the doctor's office for your yearly physical, the FedEx delivery guy walks in snapping on rubber gloves.

This week, I switched places with Mr. Redd and watched his fourth graders. A lot of his kids were in my class last year, and it's refreshing to know that they haven't matured one bit since they were third graders.

We gave the kids a BM each morning this week; first reading, then math, then science, then social studies. Let me tell you, standing around for two hours every day with nothing to do but watch kids take a test is like Christmas coming early.

Mr. Redd left a page of observations on my desk after each test. Among the gems:

"Joaqim counting on his fingers... during the READING test! Probably counting up his IQ points. Who is this kid?"

"Lakeisha filled in a bubble on all 50 lines of the Scantron answer sheet. She did this without even opening her test booklet, so she never noticed that there were only 20 questions on the test."

"Suzie must have pulled an all-nighter, because she fell asleep at 8:30."

I went through the math tests and found many of them to be in almost pristine condition. Most of the kids showed no work at all. Maybe Franco has been spreading the word about his "new way" of doing math.

You'd think that the kids would understand that the way we practice solving math problems in class is the way they should solve math problems on a test. I mean, Lebron James doesn't shoot jump shots in practice but then try to kick the ball through the hoop during a game. A concert pianist doesn't sweep her trained fingers across the keys in rehearsal only to pound out a sonata with her elbows at the recital.

Never once in class have we scanned a problem, grabbed the first two numbers we saw, added them up in our heads, and then picked the answer that's closest. However, that appears to be exactly what some of my kids did on the math benchmark.

Many of the wrong answers chosen didn't even make sense

mathematically. A boy with only 17 apples somehow gave 34 apples to a friend. A 24 page comic book will take 36 days to read. 56 boys and 37 girls were selling popcorn, yet the total number of kids was only 19. I'm sure that if 21 had been an answer choice for that one, 50% of my kids would have chosen it.

Then there were the questions that make me despise the BM-producers. Two division questions, when we clearly haven't even introduced the concept yet. One question that I had to create an algebraic system of equations to solve – on a third grade test!!

And this little turd of diabolical cruelty:
"Tommy is taking folklorien class. His lesson begins at the time shown on the clock below. What time does Tommy's folklorien class begin?"

FOLKLORIEN??!!?? What the folklorien is a folklorien???

The question just required the kids to read an analog clock, but instead, it totally hung them up on a word that hasn't been used, outside of Renaissance Fairs, for a couple of centuries!

The kids' mistakes on the science test were much more fun to read. By "fun," I of course mean "depressing."

The bubble gum hypothesis question did indeed show up on the test, and I was happy that we had performed it in advance so the kids would be prepared. But then I checked the tests and saw that only half the kids got it right. Gwenn chose "the mass of the bubble gum will change color."

The majority of my kids decided that a short-sleeve shirt and sandals would be the best attire for an outdoors science investigation. Twelve children would use a ruler or a stopwatch to measure the temperature of melting chocolate. Six of my students believe that a magnet can attract a cardboard box. Most confounding of all was a question that asked which action would be CORRECT to do during an investigation, where three of my students, I kid you not, chose "Decide not to tell your teacher about a small cut on your finger."

Clearly, we have a lot of work to do this year. I suppose the benchmarks did serve some purpose after all, in much the same way that a car's gas gauge shows when the tank is empty. Obviously, we need to look more closely at test strategies. Because if we have another set of BMs like this, I might just smash my folklorien in anger.
Later,

Ben Shmarkstink

Date: Monday, October 12, 2009
To: Fred Bommerson
From: Jack Woodson
Subject: We're gonna potty like it's 1999!

Hey buddy,

Let me answer your questions about the science BM in the order that you asked.

1)   Ascot and speedo was NOT one of the answer choices.
2)   It shouldn't matter if the ruler was metric or customary – it won't measure temperature!
3)   The question never said there was a hunk of iron inside the cardboard box.
4)   We don't (officially) teach the "suck it up" mentality here, so nobody should have chosen that answer.

Enjoy your trip to New York! I know that might be hard to do since most of your time will be spent in meetings, AND because you'll be with Larry and Philby. But if you get a chance, try to see Mount Rushmore. And the Golden Gate Bridge. And whatever else might be up in that area.

OK, I realize now that Isabel might not really have been geographically-challenged when she told me she was moving to Miami last week; she might have been making a joke. Nah, she was confused.

Moving from confused to dazed, the funniest thing happened this morning. On my way from the office to pick up my kids, I stopped to use one of the student bathrooms, which is usually empty at that time of the morning. Today, however, I was not alone.

I was standing at one of the urinals, doing my business when this little kindergartener walked in and went to the one right next to me. Clearly, no one has ever explained to him the rules of male restroom etiquette.

I've seen this kid before and taken notice because he's short even by kindergarten standards. I'd be surprised if he was 3 feet tall.

It all happened very quickly. The kid stepped up and yanked his pants down around his ankles. He couldn't have peed more than two drops and he was done. Then he sneezed.

Some combination of the sneeze, the lowered pants, and the simultaneous fart knocked the kid down. He actually fell to the floor, sort of backwards and sideways.

The poor kid was rolling around, trying to right himself like a turtle that's been flipped over, and all I could do was try my very best not to bust a gut from laughing.

I eventually had to reach down, pick the kid up, and get him set upright once again. I asked if he was OK (still fighting back giggles), but he didn't seem to hear me. He looked like a flash-bang grenade had been set off in front of him, and he swayed drunkenly on his feet with a dazed look on his face. Then suddenly he snapped out of it. He pulled up his pants, yelled, "BYE!" and made a beeline for the door.

"You might want to wash your... OK then, never mind," I trailed off as he disappeared.

The rest of my day was pretty uneventful, but the events of the morning reminded me of something that I don't think I told you about last week.

Last Tuesday, Cerulean's mother came up to the school to deliver a doctor's note.

Cerulean is a large girl who's just not very bright and who takes so many bathroom breaks that we've had to call home, concerned. Thus, the doctor's note. It made for a very interesting read, though some of the technical jargon was a bit over my head.

The note said:

"Cerulean has a functional voiding disturbance which has strained the bladder so that she has trouble with wetness, holding urine. Please allow the child to go to the bathroom when she feels the need and encourage her to stay as long as it takes her to completely empty her bladder. Your cooperation with this is sincerely appreciated."

"Functional voiding disturbance??!!?" What on earth is that? While I'm sure Dave Barry would say that would make a great name for a rock band, it sounds to me like one of those dire side effects that are always listed with prescription medication.

"Possible side effects of Drugzinol include cotton mouth, snow blindness, explosive flatulence, and functional voiding disturbance."

I also noticed that we are asked to encourage Cerulean to stay as long as it takes her to completely empty her bladder. I guess whenever she's using the bathroom, I should stand outside the door with pom-poms, cheering, "Push it out, push it out, WAAAAAY out!"

Truly, I don't begrudge someone an actual medical issue. But Cerulean is the kind of girl who will most definitely take advantage of this. She was in Mrs. Bird's room when the note was delivered, and coincidentally enough, she needed to use the bathroom as soon as her mother had left. It wasn't even 8:30! Wednesday, she raised her hand to ask me around 2:00, and she got up and slowly walked past the other kids, grinning and smirking at them like she was on her way to accept the crown for prom queen.

There's already another girl in my afternoon class, Temperance, who presented a similar doctor's note at the beginning of the year. So each afternoon, it's become a contest to see which of them will ask first. Not which one will ask – which one will ask FIRST. This afternoon, after both of them had gone and returned, Tyler told me that he needed to go. Unfortunately for him, he didn't have a doctor's note, so his request was denied. Fortunately for me, he didn't break wind and blow himself out of his chair. I think that would have trumped any doctor's note.

Talk to you later,

Gus T. Kidd

Date: Wednesday, October 14, 2009
To: Fred Bommerson
From: Jack Woodson
Subject: Playing for the wrong team

Hey dude,

OK, you are either a genius or the craziest fruitcake on the planet. It's not enough that you worked the phrase "functional voiding disturbance" into conversation during your customer meeting yesterday, but you did it THREE TIMES???

The funniest part about that (or the saddest maybe) is that your clients just nodded their heads as if they knew what you were talking about. I guess it does sound like a legitimate semiconductor malfunction. Still, I would have loved to have been there to see Larry's and Philby's reactions as you introduced the newest jargon into play.

Get your customers to start using that term in their correspondence with you, and drinks are on me next time we hang out.

One of my kids used a new term today, but I don't think he was just being a smart-alec. I had a conversation with Kevin this morning that introduced me to the brand new word AND made me fearful of ever having children in this lifetime.

After finishing his problem of the day, Kevin (AKA Anferny) called me over to tell me that he had a football game coming up on Friday night. I made a little small talk with him, asking how he liked football and what position he played. He then told me that they were playing a team called the Dragons.

I said, "Oooh, they sound dangerous. What's the name of YOUR team?"

He replied, "The Mancocks."

While a circuit within my brain suddenly burst into flame and began to smoke, my mouth filled in as best it could. Trying to relate it to the unfortunately chosen South Carolina mascot, I asked, "Oh, is that a type of bird?"

Kevin responded, "No, it's just a name my coach likes."

"And has your coach registered with the proper authorities yet?" That's what I might have asked if I didn't have such tremendous self-control. Instead, I wittily responded, "Ahhhh."

Later in the day, when I had a free moment during my planning period, I looked up "mancock" online. After skimming past forty or so entries for adult sites that might get me fired just for reading the web addresses, I finally found one that defined a mancock as "a type of birch bark container used to store rice in some villages."

Poor fire-breathing, scaly Dragons... You don't stand a chance against the wooden, grain-filled Mancocks.

I'll admit, that word haunted me for the entire morning. But it was put out of my mind for a while by another incident right before lunch.

About fifteen minutes before picking the kids up from the gym, I walked up to the office to check my mailbox. As I passed the cafeteria, where all of the kindergarten kids were filing in to have their lunch, I heard a sudden wailing. In the space of one footstep, a mighty debate that Gollum himself would have been proud of raged inside my mind.

"Do I stop and render assistance?"
"No, it's kindergarten, let them handle it. Don't get involved."
"Well, I've already glanced at the scene of the crime, I shouldn't just keep walking."
"You can always say you thought the screeching was coming from a rabid possum loose in the cafeteria."
"Oh hey, it's the little kid who sneezed/farted and blew himself down in the bathroom. I wonder why he continues to scream like somebody's attached electrodes to his groin?"

In the end, I forced myself to respect the Good Samaritan Law (you can't witness an accident and drive on past without checking on the situation), and I went over to see what was going on. A small crowd of kids was gathered around my tiny friend, who was writhing on the floor and showing no signs of lowering the volume on his shrieks. I zeroed in on the calmest looking kid, a boy who looked like he was annoyed that the lunch line had come to a halt, and I asked him to tell me what had happened. The boy pointed down at the kid on the ground and said, "He hit me."

Yeah, that's usually the response when you hit someone, you keel over and scream incessantly. After a few minutes of interrogation, I discovered that the boy on the ground had slapped the other boy on the butt, so THAT boy turned around and kicked the first kid in the junk. Hard, judging by his continued caterwauling.

It's a shame that he didn't add, "It's for science," because then I would have felt justified in letting it go. Instead, I had to wait for a Kindergarten teacher to show up and take control. When she asked what happened, I told her that the poor little guy got kicked in the mancock.

Her eyes widened, but all she said was, "Oh!" So I added, "Also, I think he may have a functional voiding disturbance."

OK, so you're not the only one who's a genius/crazy fruit-cake.

Yours truly,

John Mancock

Date: Friday, October 16, 2009
To: Fred Bommerson
From: Jack Woodson
Subject: They call me MISTER Teacher

Dude,

I don't care if one definition of mancock is "the awesomest source of awesomeness in the universe" – you don't name a Pee Wee football team something so close to something so anatomically private! I'm worried about the league Kevin is playing in. It wouldn't surprise me at all if his next matchups are against the Titmouses, the Spotted Dicks, and the Golden Taints.

Ugh. Now I feel the need to take a shower again. Let's move off of weird team names and on to weird kids.

I have a little girl in my class this year, Shelly, who doesn't quite seem all there. She's a sweet enough little girl, and so far, she appears to be doing all right academically. However, there are frequently times when I talk to her face to face, and I can tell that the light is on, but nobody's home.

One major issue, she ALWAYS calls me "Miss Woodson." She's not being malicious or trying to cut me down, she just feels for some reason that that's what she should call me. When I try to explain to her that I am a man, and therefore I should be addressed as "Mister," she gets a puzzled look on her face, as if I was telling her that Santa Claus and the Tooth Fairy were not real.

I thought for a while that perhaps Shelly called everyone Miss and was completely unfamiliar with any other prefix. But that was disproven a couple of days into the school year. The art teacher and I were monitoring the drop-off zone out in front of the school when Shelly's aunt pulled up and let her out. Shelly ran past us yelling, "Good morning, Mister Vann! Good morning, Miss Woodson!!"

Maybe it's just me, though I do consider myself to be somewhat manly looking. I mean, my Adam's apple is as prominent as the next guy's, and I rock a mean three-day stubble. I don't think that she actually views me as a female. So I'm at a loss as to why she can't understand why I wouldn't be MISTER Woodson.

I can just imagine what would happen if I lined up with a bunch of people with various jobs and let Shelly greet all of us.

"Good morning, Mister Ramsey!

Good morning, Doctor Barton!
Good morning, Judge Carson!
Good morning, Special Agent Johnson!
Good morning, Archduke Fielder!
Good morning, Miss Woodson!"

This afternoon, I noticed that Shelly was writing notes at her desk while we were going over the homework. When I told her that she needed to be paying attention and grading along with us, she looked shocked and replied, "But I was writing a note to YOU!"

She said this very defensively, as if she was thinking, "When we walked into class today, our two choices were to either pay attention and do the work or to daydream and write notes – and I made my choice!"

I told her that it was very sweet of her, but that she needed to do that at home, not during math class. Still affronted, she continued, "It's a note about how you're my favorite teacher!"

I glanced quickly at the paper on her desk and saw little hearts lining the edges. At that moment, I was very thankful that I hadn't just snatched the paper off of her desk and thrown it away, because I could totally imagine Shelly tearfully asking, "Miss Woodson, why? Why do you hate love?"

I finally convinced her to stop writing notes and to pay attention in class – at least, her version of paying attention.

At any rate, I'll probably be getting a very lovely note come Monday morning along the lines of, "You're the best, Miss Woodson!!"

Talk to you later,

Matt Skewlin

Date:	Tuesday, October 20, 2009
To:	Fred Bommerson
From:	Jack Woodson
Subject:	Commercial success

Hey bud,

Good to have you back in Dallas, with most of your sanity intact after a week with Larry. I know how exhausted you must be after spending most of yesterday catching up on paperwork, build statuses, team updates, and the like. Yet somehow you found the time to tell everyone about that last email.

They all sent me emails calling me Miss or Ms. Except Winter, who always has to top everyone. His email was addressed to Mademoiselle Woodson. And they say engineers never have an original thought.

In addition to those emails, guess what I received yesterday? If you said an autographed picture of veteran character actor Robert Loggia, you're not far off. I got (pause for dramatic effect) A CARD FROM SHELLY!!

Who could possibly have seen that one coming?

It said, "Dear Msr Woodsman, You are the best techer ever! Love, Shelly."

I'm willing to overlook the misspelling of my name, since she does verbally say Woodson. So I won't need to call her "Barry" in return.

I think "Msr" is just a misspelling as well and doesn't mean that she's decided to start addressing me as Monsignor. She still looks at me oddly when I ask her to call me "Mister," but she's not the only one who is still trying to figure me out. I've been with my kids for about two months now, and it's amazing how the two classes behave as completely separate microcosms. One group seems to really "get" me, while the other seems to wonder what planet I'm from.

This morning, we were going over a word problem that mentioned someone's garden. I knew that Mrs. Bird had just finished reading a story with the children called "Ugly Vegetables," so after reading the word problem, I said, "Tim's garden is 5 feet wide. Oh, maybe Tim is planting some UGLY VEGETABLES!"

Dead silence. I looked out into a sea of blank faces, as a tumbleweed slowly drifted across the room. I tapped on the end of my overhead marker and spoke into it – "Is this thing on?"

After lunch, with my second class, I tried the exact same bit. Maybe it's just the personalities of the different kids, maybe I improved the timing in my comedy act, or maybe the cafeteria pizza pockets had nitrous oxide in them, but the results were decidedly different.

"Tim's garden is 5 feet wide. Oh, hey, I'll bet Tim is planting some UGLY VEGETABLES!"

The room exploded into laughter and applause like Showtime at the Apollo. Kids were waving towels in circles around their heads, shouting "WOO WOO!" and throwing buckets of confetti at each other.

Different strokes for different folks, I suppose.

They may not all be hanging on every word I say just yet, but they certainly are influenced by what they see on television. Mrs. Bird told us a story over lunch today about a response she got from Jacob during her social studies lesson. She's been discussing the court system with the class and going over the roles and functions of judges, juries, lawyers, etc. Today she asked, "Who could you go to if you needed help in solving a legal problem?"

Jacob immediately raised his hand and shouted out, "James Handler, The Dallas Sledgehammer!"

Clearly, Handler's local commercials – "My neighbor's dog peed on my mailbox, and James Handler got me $450,000!!" – have made an impression on young Jacob, among others.

This is not the first advertising campaign that has had an effect in the classroom. A few years ago, every time I mentioned bar graphs, one little boy would go into a robotic trance and recite, "Cingular – Raising the bar!"

Heck, Mrs. Fitzgerald and I have been paying homage to an ancient commercial for years! You remember the old jingle, "Cha cha cha, Charmin!" for Charmin toilet paper? We adapted that to make it easy for the kids to remember where to place the comma in a number. "Cha cha cha, comma!" (Where each "cha" is a digit to bypass.)

I'm always tempted to tell the kids, "Don't squeeze the Thousands!"

There is no possible way that these kids are familiar with the old Charmin commercials, yet the jingle resonates with them. It makes me wonder if teachers might not be wise to take a different approach to lesson planning. Maybe we should start making commercials to be aired during Saturday morning cartoons and Monday night wrestling. This might turn out to be more effective in promoting concepts like estimation and the scientific method than boring ol' classroom activities.

I'm thinking a simple, direct message played over and over for 30 seconds, wedged in between ads for Playstation games and Vytorin. Just look at how successfully the phrase, "Headon, apply directly to the forehead!" has gotten stuck in our brains. Sure, everyone wishes they could meet the creator of that ad, just so they could punch him in the face, but there's no denying that the message sticks.

We could record someone saying, "Comma! Apply directly between the Hundreds and the Thousands. Comma!"

Over and over, for the entire commercial.

I mean, if James Handler can infiltrate my kids' minds with a catchy slogan, then I sure as heck ought to be able to!

Later,

Mark Etting

Date: Thursday, October 22, 2009
To: Fred Bommerson
From: Jack Woodson
Subject: Green Eggs and Math

Hey Fred,

OK, if we ever DO get the green light to shoot commercials, tell Tiffany I'm putting her in charge. Her idea of "Division – So easy, a 3rd grader could do it" is genius!!

Larry's proposal – "Just glue it" – Not so much.

The fridge in my kitchen finally has some modern art displayed! Jacob gave me a hand-drawn picture today, which was very sweet of him. It was a picture of Larry the Cucumber from the cartoon Veggie Tales. My nephew Kyle loves Veggie Tales, so I'm familiar with some of the characters.

I did find it just a bit inappropriate, though, that Jacob had depicted Larry The Cucumber wearing nothing but a thong. I mean, I've never heard of a cucumber hammock.

No, I'm just kidding. Larry was dressed as Sherlock Holmes – there shall be no obscene vegetable portraits on my kitchen appliances!

Jacob gave me the picture right before leaving my room this morning, around 10:30. At 10:50, the class went to music, and from there to lunch.

When we went to pick the kids up from the cafeteria, Jacob was visibly upset, as was Nestor (favorite color: OGO).

While Mrs. Bird took the other kids outside for recess, I tried to get to the bottom of the mystery (as I'm sure Sherlock Cucumber would have done).

Somehow Mickey was involved in this whole mess as well, and he seemed more than happy to tell me what had happened.

"Jacob told me he didn't want to be friends with Nestor anymore, and when I told Nestor, he started crying. Then Nestor said he didn't want to be friends with Jacob anymore, and when I said that to Jacob, HE started crying."

I thanked Mickey, The Great Facilitator, and then asked him to go away. Nicely, of course.

Left with Jacob and Nestor, I proceeded into the classic "If you can't say anything nice, don't say anything at all" speech (AKA, The Bronze Rule, copyright 815 B.C.). I pointed out that if neither of them had made mean comments, neither of them would have had to cry and feel bad.

At that, Jacob, on the verge of tears again, turned to Nestor and exclaimed, in his high-pitched voice, "I'm so sorry! Can you ever forgive me?"

Nestor responded by throwing his arms around Jacob in a full-on bear hug, complete with back thumping.

I couldn't help but think that somewhere, Chris Farley and John Belushi were smiling.

I told Mrs. Bird that I would take her homeroom to the library this afternoon so they could check out a couple of new books. As they were making their selections, I noticed that Nestor had a book that was way beyond his level. I asked Mrs. Drogz, the librarian, if she had any really, really, REALLY basic books that he could read. The first thing that came to mind was Dick and Jane. She returned shortly with a Dr. Seuss book which I thought would be perfect.

Nestor's face lit up, and he exclaimed, "Oh, I know that one!" He pointed at the title and proudly traced the words with his finger as he read, "The. Cat. In. The. Hat."

It was very touching to see Nestor so excited, and I didn't have the heart to point out that the book was actually titled "Hop on Pop." But at least he recognized the author, so that's something, right?

In a showing that all was once again right with the world, Jacob started helping Nestor sound out the words in the book. Their lunchroom tiff seemed to be a thing of the past, and I kept an eye on Mickey to make sure he stayed away from them.

I had another Dr. Seuss moment while grading today's tests after school. The final question was a written response question, and it asked, "Give an example of when you would round instead of using exact numbers. Explain."

As usual, answers ranged from mostly right to inexplicably wrong to downright unintelligible. I was looking for answers that contained any mention of what we had discussed when we first started rounding, namely, going to the store and keeping track of the total cost. Probably about 1/3 of the kids got this.

Eddie, Lex, and a few other lazy kids answered, "at school," or, "in math."

Gwenn really took the WHEN to heart and answered, "Monday, Tuesday, Thursday, Friday."

I guess Wednesdays are rounding-free days for priti prinseses?

Franco and Hillary both wrote, "Never. You wouldn't get an answer."

Great! So glad they think my class is all about learning things that have no use whatsoever! Tomorrow, I'll teach them how to make piggy banks out of Kleenex.

This brings us to the Seussical response. Ava's answer to when you would round was, "At my house, in the car, in a tree, at the school."

For some reason, after I read this, my mind immediately started chanting,

"I will not round that in a car,
 I will not round that with a jar.
 I will not round that in a box,
 I will not round that with a fox."

I think I'm going to start requiring these free response answers to be written in rhyme. And maybe illustrated with vegetables that can talk.
Talk to you later,

Sham-I-Am

Date: Wednesday, October 28, 2009
To: Fred Bommerson
From: Jack Woodson
Subject: Talk this way

Hey Fred,

You're absolutely right, kids like Nestor are tough cases. He can't read, he doesn't do math well, he can barely count, and he's actually too low academically to be in the special education program. He's certainly not going to pass the TAKS test, which is the end-all measuring tool for the state. Unfortunately, the TAKS tests measure the growth of a student about as much as the height stick at an amusement park measures growth.

When I worked at Six Flags in high school, we would put the height stick (a 5-foot long ruler with a crossbar set at the minimum height) down next to any child we wanted to check and give it a twirl. If it whacked the kid in the head, he was tall enough to ride. It certainly didn't measure how much the kid had grown over the summer, though.

There is no chance at all that the TAKS is going to whack Nestor in the head, so to speak. So he will show up as a failure blip on my records. I've accepted that. It doesn't mean he's going to leave my class without making any progress, though. The important thing now is to get him to a higher level than he is now, even if that level is far below the third grade requirements.

Hey, he can already count twice as high as he could on that first day, and more importantly, he doesn't throw letters into the mix anymore. Having him partnered up with Jacob is very helpful, because they can work together, and Nestor can feel some sense of accomplishment. Plus, I've heard them have some pretty good discussions during science time.

That's more than I can say for some of the other pairings.

This year, the district has made a really big point of stressing what they call "Accountable Talk" among the children. This means that the kids are supposed to explain in detail how they got their answers and discuss their strategies in depth with the other students.

This can be quite the challenge for many of my kids, since they are used to just saying a number when I ask a question or shouting, "NOOO!" at another kid when they disagree with his or her answer.

Frequently, I will say, "Please raise your hand if you know the answer," and 20 hands will shoot up. But when I add, "AND if you can explain to me how you got your answer," 17 of those hands go back down.

As a reminder and an aid, each desk has a list of accountable talk prompts taped to it to help the kids remember how to begin. These prompts include:

"I got my answer by _____."
"To solve this problem, first I _____, then I _____."
"I'd like to add more to what _____ said."

To be honest, my kids very rarely begin their sentences any of these ways. However, the two prompts that they really DO seem to have latched on to are the ones that begin, "I agree with _____," and, "I disagree with _____."

It was very funny to hear the way in which these prompts came into play this afternoon.

The kids were completing a name graph in their math journals. To construct this bar graph, we had to first create a tally chart that showed the number of letters in people's first names. I was standing at the center of the class asking the kids to raise their hands if they had 4 letters in their first name, 5 letters in their first name, etc.

When I got to the "10 or more" category, only Thilleenica raised her hand, saying she had 11 letters in her name.

With our tally chart completed, we moved on to the next step, but that's when DaQuayvius raised his hand and said, "I disagree with Thilleenica, because I counted the letters in her name, and there are only 10 letters in her name."

Immediately, Thilleenica raised her hand and retorted, "I disagree with DaQuayvius, because I KNOW how to spell my own name, and there are 11 letters in my name."

Let no one say that my kids aren't talking accountably! Though my newest little girl, Fo'lina, doesn't want to talk to me at all. Fo'lina showed up last week, and her mom raved and raved about what a fantastic reader she was. That day, though, before entering my classroom, Fo'lina asked, "Do I have to read in this class?"

Mrs. Bird told me later that she had been asked the exact same question. I was tempted to use some accountable talk of my own – "I disagree with your mother."

This morning, Mrs. Bird told me that she had asked Fo'lina to bring a book about sharks over to me yesterday, but that Fo'lina had hesitantly replied, "Can someone else go with me?"

When Mrs. Bird asked her why she needed someone to escort her ten feet across the hall, she answered, "I'm scared of Mr. Woodson."

I considered donning a hockey mask and walking into Mrs. Bird's room, shouting, "FO'LINA!! WHY ARE YOU AFRAID OF ME? BRING ME THAT BOOK! NOW!!"

But that would be cruel. And while I may be scary to some, I'm really not cruel.

While we were switching classes, Mickey shared some accountable talk of his own with another hilarious insight. As soon as he saw Mrs. Bird, who was wearing a horizontally-striped black and white long-sleeve shirt, he told her, "You look like one of those guys who goes…"

Here he proceeded to stick both hands out and pretend he was pushing on an invisible wall.

Brilliant.

Talk to you later,

Marcel Marshow'n'tell

Date: Friday, October 30, 2009
To: Fred Bommerson
From: Jack Woodson
Subject: A Jack of all grades

Hey Fred,

Here's hoping that the first grader who ran into me at full speed out by the buses today learns to watch where he's going. And that he recovers from his injuries quickly.

I haven't really kept in touch with Philby since I left HPU, so I'm sorry I can't help you out with whatever issues you two are having now. At least not directly. Give him a little space, and hopefully things will blow over. I'd agree that it's always good to maintain clear communication, but I don't think my sample Accountable Talk prompts are going to help you much. Especially not if you fill them in like MadLibs.

"To solve this problem, first I shaved Philby bald, then I laughed my butt off" – made ME laugh, but it's not going to resolve your dispute.

Let's accountably talk about the blessings of ADHD. I'm speaking, of course, of Big Jack, and the wonderful world of Shangri-La-La he lives in. This is a boy who routinely asks me after tests, "Is a 50 good?" To which I have to routinely bite my tongue and NOT reply, "No, Jack, in fact, it's so bad that I'm pretty sure it's going to start raining soon because a 50 usually makes the angels cry."

The other day, tired of the kids repeatedly asking how old I am, I tried to show them that they could find anyone's age if they knew the current year and the year of that person's birth. Since most of my students were born in 2000, I put 2009 and 2000 on the board and asked what we should do with these numbers. Big Jack immediately shouted, "ADD!!"

So, I added 2009 and 2000 and then complimented Big Jack on looking quite well-preserved for someone over 4,000 years old. He just grinned and asked, "Is that good?"

Yesterday, I had to keep him and a couple of others in my room during PE because they did not finish their work during class time. As is so often the case, Big Jack weighed the options of labeling fractions vs. playing rocket ship with his pencils, and the fractions were found wanting.

As a result, we were both in my room when Mrs. Fitzgerald's voice suddenly boomed in from the PA system. She must not have realized that I had kids in the room, because she didn't address me as "Mr. Woodson," but rather used my first name.

When he heard, "Jack, are you there?" coming from on high, Big Jack immediately looked up and responded, "YES!"

He must have thought God was speaking directly to him, rescuing him from having to finish his work.

"Did I do good, God?"

He actually DID do pretty good on today's test, which was taken from the math textbook. Once again, the final question was a free response, giving the kids a chance to show how poorly they can express themselves in written English. After reading a couple of answers, I decided to make that question an extra credit question.

It read, "A cake has been cut into 40 pieces. Is it reasonable to say that this is enough cake for 32 people?"

If the kids said anything to the extent that yes, it is reasonable because there are more pieces of cake than there are people, I gave them 1 point extra credit. If they expressed their rationale even more clearly, I gave them 2 points.

Big Jack wrote, "No, it does not make sense because the people would get 1 piece only and sometimes I want to eat 2 pieces of cake or 3."

I gave the lad 2 extra credit points! It wasn't at all the answer I was looking for, but he did explain his thinking quite clearly, and being a cake lover myself, I couldn't exactly disagree with him.

I even made it a point to write, "You did good, Jack" on the top of his test. He'll still come and ask me if he did good, even after getting his test back, but now I'll at least have something to point to. Have a great Halloween!

High Jack

Date: Monday, November 2, 2009
To: Fred Bommerson
From: Jack Woodson
Subject: The Nightmare after Halloween

Hey dude,

I had no doubt that once I told you a little more about Big Jack, he would begin to remind you just a bit of the person with whom you share a cubicle wall. The ADHD, the proclivity for sweets, the always speaking before ever thinking.

I hope you had a fantastic Halloween. It's a shame Nancy hasn't thrown one of her costume parties in a while, but I had a good time answering the door at my house, seeing all the little tykes in their twilight finery. I went all out myself, dressing as Wolverine of the X-Men, only instead of claws, I taped three sharpened pencils to each of my hands.

My house was popular! And in case you were wondering, I was handing out the good stuff, my friend. We're talking Twix, Nestle Crunch, and Jolly Ranchers! None of this knockoff stuff. Mrs. Bird was telling me last week that she usually goes to the dollar store and comes away with a bunch of cheap imitator brand candy. I'm sure her neighbor's kids were thrilled to receive n&n's, Slickers, and Two Musketeers.

This year, I followed through on my plan to be a bit more discriminatory in who got the good stuff.

I really get a kick out of seeing 5-year-old superheroes and 4-foot tall Transformers. What I do NOT enjoy is the roving bands of teenagers who come in no perceivable disguise, knock on the door, and mutely hold out a pillow case. They don't even go to the effort of saying, "Trick or Treat!"

In the past, I've tried reasoning with them. "Um, you have no costume." – No reasoning to be had.

I've tried sarcasm on them. "Oooh, I can see you're going for angry punk! Nailed it!" – Sarcasm wasted.

I've tried shaming them. "Um, you have no costume." – Zilch on the shame-o-meter.

This year, I decided to hit 'em where it hurts. Right in the taste buds.

I went out and bought a bag of candy corn. I know there are some people out there who love candy corn (including Larry and Big Jack, no doubt), but personally, I think it is one of the most disgusting food items on the planet, second only to those really nasty orange circus peanuts that have the look, feel, and taste of Styrofoam packing peanuts.

On Saturday night, whenever a cute little costumed kid came to my door, I happily placed a Twix or a Jolly Rancher into his or her bag. But whenever it was a lazy teen, looking to capitalize on October 31st, he received one single candy corn.

Boom goes the dynamite.

One kid, dressed perfectly like an extra from a high school-set movie that does not take place on Halloween, stared at me in shock and said, "That's it??"

"That's all you're dressed for," was my reply.

I almost added, "The good candy is for Top Performers only." A tip of the hat to Latya, who would never turn the A/C in his car up all the way when he drove the gang to lunch. According to him, the highest setting was for Top Performers only.

I'd say I passed out about fifteen candy corns on Saturday night. I'm sure as heck not going to eat the rest of them. Maybe I'll save the bag for next year, so lazy teens can get one single STALE candy corn!

On a completely unrelated note, if you know of anyone there who has a recommendation for the best way to get toilet paper out of trees, please let me know.

Several kids greeted me this morning by telling me about their Halloween experiences, their costumes, and all the candy they had scored. I heard about ghosts, Batmen, princesses, and Power Rangers, to name a few. Katie and Ava gave me Hershey's Kisses as soon as they saw me.

Then Gwenn walked into the room, and the whole class gasped in horror. She (or someone she knows) had shaved both of her eyebrows off. I have no idea whether or not this was related in any way to Halloween. She may have just decided that November was anti-brow month for all I know. One thing's for certain, though. The lack of eyebrows does NOT make her priti-er.

After lunch, when I started to grade the bell ringer with my second class, Victor suddenly spoke up and announced, "Saturday night, after trick-or-treating, we went home, and my mom was real tired, and she fell asleep on the couch, and she didn't cook us dinner, and I was hungry, and so I had no choice but to eat all my candy. It was good!"

Good ol' Victor. Chooses not to do his homework, but has no choice whatsoever when it comes to stuffing himself full of sugar before bedtime.

Here's hoping the class-wide sugar high wears off by mid-week, so I can actually accomplish some teaching! Those rulers aren't going to measure themselves!

Later,

Admiral Candy Cornelius Vanderbilt

Date:	Thursday, November 5, 2009
To:	Fred Bommerson
From:	Jack Woodson
Subject:	Behold the power of cheese

Hey buddy,

Tell Tiffany she can NOT have my leftover candy corns and that I'm doing her a huge favor. Weirdo.

Tom Winter sent me a five-paragraph essay extolling the virtues of those orange Styrofoam peanut candies. Don't you guys ever do any work over there? I'm guessing not, since I also received several photographs of the Heat Pumps gang with no eyebrows. Including one of ME!! Why is my ID mug shot still on the HPU server?

Anyway, today was a beating of a day. Here I was all set to give my students the gift that is perimeter and area, but the schedule kept getting upset by interruptions. Never mind the fact that it rained all day long, so there was no outdoor recess. I can live with that. Sure, the kids get cabin fever and act like they don't know left from right, up from down, or isotropic from anisotropic. But then I lost about an hour of class time due to two mandatory out-of-the-classroom treks.

First thing in the morning, I had to take my homeroom to another classroom so that they could do hearing tests. It's very interesting how the kids can hear a minute little beep that tells them when to raise their hand, yet somehow they don't hear me when I tell them to write their names on tests. Amazingly, Eddie was able to raise his hand at the beep without hearing his own name first.

I asked the nurse if it was wrong of me to tell kids who have trouble listening to "go home, get a really big spoon, and scoop all of the dirt out of your ears."

She politely said, "Um..."

The second time loss came after lunch, when the entire 3rd and 4th grades crowded into the auditorium to listen to our counselor, Miss Rooker, talk to them about the dangers of a new drug going around local schools. This assembly was called after our Monday staff meeting (now weekly, for our pleasure!), in which a district spokesperson came and talked to us about cheese.

I'm not talking about your typical individually-wrapped slices of processed Velveeta. This is "Cheese," the new designer drug that is sweeping the halls of Dallas-area schools.

To my knowledge, we haven't had much of a drug problem at my school, except for the one time three years ago when a 5th grader allegedly brought in 20-some grams of marijuana. I imagine he tried to roll it up into a big construction paper doobie, but I didn't actually witness this. Frankly, I'm just glad I haven't had any kids watch Scarface at home and then come in and try to snort a line of Play-doh off their desk. (Say hello to my little backpack!)

Nevertheless, this new drug, cheese, is already a major problem at middle and high schools, and people are worried it will filter down into elementary schools. Cheese is a combination of black tar heroin and crushed Tylenol PM – two great tastes that taste great together! I can practically see the Colombian drug lords sitting around their compounds, going about their business, when suddenly –

"Hey! You got your Tylenol PM in my black tar heroin!"
"Hey! You got your black tar heroin in my Tylenol PM!"

Cheese follows in the footsteps of last year's scare – Pepto Bismol and liquid ecstasy (codename: Pickles). Rumor has it that a new threat is on the horizon – a hybrid mixture of flour, methamphetamines, and oatmeal termed "Sesame Seed Bun."

I can't for the life of me imagine why anyone would even want to go near a drug called Cheese, but then I could never understand the appeal of edible cheddar-flavored product you can spray from a can – and look at the success of Cheez Whiz!

Apparently, Cheese is sold in tiny increments called "bumps" which are snorted, often with the ink straw from a ballpoint pen. Except in Plano, where they no doubt use rolled up hundred dollar bills. We were also told that some kids may hide a small amount in a Kleenex and then snort it while pretending to blow their nose. Often right at the front of the classroom! Since we were told that one of the symptoms of Cheese is euphoria, I've been advising everyone to be on guard against kids who get REALLY happy when they clear their sinuses.

Logically, we would discuss this subject with our own homerooms in our own classrooms, so that we could ensure that everyone was listening, and so we could answer any questions.

Instead, we were instructed to herd two entire grades at a time into the auditorium and do the talks there. So instead of 16-22 kids reasonably well behaved, we had roughly 250 kids closely spaced and much more interested in talking to kids they usually don't see.

Miss Rooker talked to the kids while the teachers tried to maintain order. She started by talking about illegal drugs, and she asked the kids to name the ones they knew. Among the responses were cocaine, X, beer, wine, weed, and spinach. You KNOW they would never let Popeye play Major League Baseball or ride the Tour De France all juiced up on Spinach.

A fourth grade girl stood up and announced that her grandfather has to blow into a straw before he can start his car in the morning, because of his drinking. This sparked a battle of one-upmanship, which concluded with another kid declaring, "Sometimes, my parents drink pot!"

At least nobody mentioned snorting vodka, injecting cigarettes, or smoking Michelob.

While patrolling the aisles, Mr. Redd passed by and whispered, "I hope she reads 'The House That Crack Built.'" This is an actual book that one of our old counselors used to read to the kids all the time. Believe me, the story was as entertaining as the title.

I can pretty much already predict that the result of all of this will be a few kids going home and telling their parents that they can't have macaroni and cheese anymore – because it will kill them.

And so, thanks to an ear check and Killer Cheese, we only covered perimeter today and did not get around to area. Maybe tomorrow we'll try to figure out the square footage of a Schlitz. Later,

Cheesed Lightnin'

Date:	Tuesday, November 10, 2009
To:	Fred Bommerson
From:	Jack Woodson
Subject:	Lookin' for sub (in all the wrong places)

Hey Fred,

If you really think Reggie is coming in to work high on Spinach every day, maybe an intervention is in order. Just watch out for the tell-tale side effects – headache, nausea, displeasing odor, and green teeth. Oh, and possible functional voiding disturbance.

I was off-campus yesterday to attend a meeting of other third grade teachers in the district. As expected, I came back to my classroom today to find a big mess and a list of complaints about the kids. It's unfortunate, but this seems to happen a lot with the substitute teachers we get. I know some fantastic subs, and whenever I plan to take a day off, I try to secure one of them. That way, I know the lesson will be taught, my things will be where I left them, and the kids will be kept in line, even if I don't specifically write, "Please do NOT let the kids make confetti out of my paper supplies and leave the room looking like a hotel suite that the Insane Clown Posse has trashed."

When we have to go to these meetings, however, we don't call our own subs, so it's a random crapshoot as to who we get. More often than not, these random subs don't follow the plans, and they let the kids get away with murder. It won't surprise me at all to someday come back to school and hear one of the kids tell me, "That strange lady kept drinking funny-smelling water from a paper bag."

I predict it will be Lakeisha or DaQuayvius, who have raised tattling to an art form.

Substitute teaching can be a difficult, thankless job. Unless you get a long-term gig, it can be hard to establish any kind of authority or relationship with the class. I know this first-hand, since I subbed for a while before getting certified.

My very first substitute teaching job was in a 7th grade science class. Ugh. Middle school – you will never find a more wretched hive of scum and villainy. And acne and raging adolescent insanity. I had five class periods, all full of hormonally supercharged raving lunatics posing in the guise of children. Loud, boisterous, pushing and shoving – and those were the GOOD ones!

The lesson plan had me giving a test over the respiratory system. Seemed nice and easy. The plan also said that the kids would almost certainly need the entire fifty minutes to complete the test, but that early finishers could read a magazine. As you might have guessed, the entire first class was finished within ten minutes. On top of that, the classroom had no magazines for these kids to read, and the kids had no books with them. The rest of the period closely resembled the pit at the New York Stock Exchange.

Thankfully, the planning period was immediately after the first period. I was bound and determined NOT to go through that ordeal four more times. I looked through this guy's cabinets and drawers, searching for any kind of activity or worksheet related to the respiratory system. If I couldn't find anything, I was prepared to have the kids make a detailed "Breathing Log."

I finally found a word search, which seemed ideal, so I quickly ran off a passel of copies. I was so proud of myself when I had something to offer the early finishers in the next period. That is, until the giggling began. That was when I took a closer look at the word search. I had noticed that it covered not only the respiratory system, but also the digestive system and the reproductive system, but in my haste, I hadn't looked at the list of words.

The very first word on the list was "anus." Further down the list, "sphincter" reared its ugly head. I'm not sure if these words represented aspects of the digestive system or the reproductive system, but I pray it was the former. At any rate, I figured the science teacher would have some fun stories when he got back the next day, and it kept the kids quiet (except for the snickers and constant whispers of, "Have you found SCROTUM yet?"). So I continued to use the worksheet for the remainder of the day.

I did leave everything the way I found it, though, which is more than I can say for my sub yesterday. I came back today to find a bag of cough drops missing from my desk and some candy from my cabinet gone. I had left very specific instructions that said the kids were beginning to work on a project but that they were NOT to draw on the poster-sized paper yet. Several completed posters were sitting on my desk.

The kids said that the sub had the radio on while they were working. I thought maybe she had played a soothing instrumental CD for them, but Smoker Anna said some guy kept talking. Sure enough, my radio dial was set to an AM talk news station. I'm sure the kids perform better when they know the ups and downs of the Dow Jones Index.

Worst of all, the sub let the kids use my electric pencil sharpener, and someone – no one will admit to it, but I'm sure it was Joaqim – put a crayon into it. Now every time I try to use it, it produces a horrendous screeching sound that makes me think somewhere, a unicorn is dying.

In the world of Wiley E. Coyote, this lady would be scientifically labeled "Substitutius non Returnus."

So my return to the classroom was slightly less than triumphant. But something pretty awesome resulted from my absence as well. There was another teacher at the meeting – well, there were LOTS of other teachers there, but not like this one. Her name is Jill, and without sounding like I've become a character from a Jane Austen novel, I'll just say she rocked my world. We weren't sitting at the same table, but I pretty much stared at her the whole time, and she occasionally glanced over at me and smiled. I could tell she liked me, and I'm pretty sure she was digging on the calculator watch.

During one of the breaks, I ventured over and introduced myself. "Hi! I'm Bright Red Tomato Face Man!" Somehow, through events I don't even recall, I got her phone number. I haven't called her yet, but I think I will this weekend.

I can tell you my respiratory system has already been affected – it's kind of hard to breathe when I think about Jill – but here's hoping my digestive and reproductive systems remain unchanged. Wish me luck!

Later,

Hot for Teacher

Date:	Thursday, November 12, 2009
To:	Fred Bommerson
From:	Jack Woodson
Subject:	Space Cadet Academy

Hey buddy,

Thank you for your overwhelming excitement that I met a girl! No, I don't have any pictures to show you! No, I'm not going to tell you her last name so you can cyber-stalk her on Facebook!

Yeah, yeah, yeah – I'll tell you what she looks like already! Larry sent me an email with one single word – "HOT??" I could practically see the drool on the monitor.

So just to get you guys off my back... Jill IS a hottie. She's about 5'4", blonde hair, blue eyes, a quick laugh, and an almost visible peppiness. She said that people tell her she looks like Reese Witherspoon, and I could see why. To my knowledge, there are no extra appendages anywhere they don't belong, she has a full set of teeth, and her voice is about as far from Fran Drescher as you could get. Nothing but pluses!!

I haven't called her yet, but like I said, I'll try over the weekend. After all, I know firsthand what her weeks are like, so I'll wait until we're not so busy.

I have to scratch the needle on the record now, slam on the brakes, and do a complete 180. Time to transition from the rose to the skunk.

I'm not sure how to put this delicately – I was feeling a bit gassy this morning. Uncontrollably gassy, apparently. At one point, as I was walking around the classroom, I pulled a one cheek sneak. I broke wind. Audibly. Not wrath of God audibly, but balloon-popping audibly.

When it happened, I glanced at Clarisa, who was sitting closest and who had a look of shock on her face. Before I could say anything, she exclaimed, "It wasn't me!"

That took me by surprise, and I asked, "Excuse me?"

She reiterated, "That was not me!"

I just nodded my head and said, "OK," as I walked away, secure in the knowledge that I had just gotten away with something. Eddie was sitting right next to Clarisa, and he SHOULD have heard it, but I guess since I didn't say his name first, he couldn't be disturbed. Nobody else was paying attention (shocker!), but if they had been, poor Clarisa would have taken the blame. After all, the universal rule is: "She who heard it, spurred it."

While we're on the subject of little farts, my young protégé, Victor, managed to do something today that few others have been able to do. He irritated me to the point of laughter. Twice!!

The first time occurred when we were grading the homework from last night. Every problem on the page involved the same steps and the same procedure. I was popcorning around the room, asking a different student to repeat the steps each time. After the first five problems, everyone seemed to have the routine down. On the tenth problem, I realized that everyone did NOT have the routine down, when I called on Victor.

Victor didn't have a clue what to do to get the answer. Big surprise. I started to chew him out, telling him that his classmates had been going over the steps for the past fifteen minutes. I ended my rant by asking, "Where have you been this whole time?!?"

His sullen, pathetic, and extremely sincere response was, "Probably on the planet Zorlon."

I shudder to think how I looked at that moment. Externally, I'm sure I looked angry and incredulous, mouth gaping wide, while internally, I was busting a gut. Long seconds ticked by as I just stared at Victor, unable to speak. Finally, I whispered, "Is that anywhere near Uranus?"

Then the giggles got out, but I masked them brilliantly with a fake coughing fit.

Later, during science class, Victor's "uniqueness" struck again. I had just asked the class how looking at an animal's teeth could tell us whether it was a carnivore or an herbivore. Several kids raised their hands, and I decided to call on Victor.

You would think that a child raising his hand is indicating that he has an answer ready to share. Quite often with my kids, however, a raised hand is merely their way of showing that they have HEARD the question, and that they are ready to begin thinking of an answer just as soon as they are called on.

This was the case with Victor. When I called his name, I could see all the signs that the gears had started slowly turning – eyes rolled back in the head, shallow breathing, soul has left the body – but no answer was forthcoming. After waiting a few agonizing moments, I started to call on somebody else, when Victor blurted, "I got nothin.'"

This time, I couldn't help laughing.

This job is so full of frustration, but then moments like this pop up and remind me of why I got into it in the first place. Laughable moments like this and the joy of farting with no consequences. It's a pretty sweet gig.
Talk to you later,

Forlorn on Zorlon

Date: Wednesday, November 18, 2009
To: Fred Bommerson
From: Jack Woodson
Subject: Beware the rise of the octagons

Hey bud,

I talked to Jill on Sunday afternoon, and we had a great conversation. Great, because it only lasted for about ten minutes, and since I've only got about fifteen minutes worth of material, I was able to save a little bit for our first date. I'm thinking we'll split a Rooty Tooty Fresh and Fruity at the IHOP, then cruise the outlet malls, ending it all with $5 worth of Donkey Kong at the arcade.

I'm kidding, of course. We actually talked for well over an hour, with none of the lulls in conversation or stinging insults that you and I seem to encounter when we talk on the phone. I'm meeting Jill on Friday evening for dinner and drinks. No IHOP, no video games. No inadvertent flatulence, no distant planets.

Hey, speaking of video games, congratulations on scoring the big new contract with Microsoft for the Xbox! I mean, I know you yourself didn't strike the deal, but that's still awesome news, and I'm more than a little jealous. The coolest project I ever got to work on while I was at HPU was the 14-pin butterfly package with insulated alfjsfpjp3jr31aafji34139redffffffffffffffffffffffffffffffffffff

Oh, sorry man! I put myself to sleep there for a second! I'll be sure to stay away from my old job Friday night!

But back to your new project, if you play your cards right, maybe you can talk your way into being used as an avatar in some new video game. They've come such a long way since we were kids, back when the characters were usually just a big square body with a circle for a head. Very simple geometry, which, as it just so happens, is our subject this week.

I've got a quiz for you. Do you know the shape of a speed limit sign? How about a railroad crossing? A stop sign?

You're correct if you said a rectangle, a circle, and not a hexagon.

I've noticed that every year, for some reason, kids are infatuated with hexagons. That is ALWAYS the first word they want to shout out when I ask them to identify any two-dimensional shape with more than four sides. I guess there really is something to be said for hex-appeal.

When I can get them to count the sides first, they are much more accurate in naming the shape. And they DO seem to know the shapes that go with those road signs. I need to find some way to get them to envision a series of street signs before choosing a name. Then maybe they would Yield their thoughts, Stop their hex addiction, and less closely resemble Slow Children at Play.

Yesterday's activity was creating two-dimensional shapes using marshmallows and toothpicks. The marshmallows were the points and the toothpicks were the line segments.

Things were going swimmingly throughout most of the class. We had covered angles, lines, rays, quadrilaterals, and all sorts of other shapes. We were nearing the end of the lesson, creating the final shape of the day, when disaster struck.

I had just asked the kids to make an 8-sided figure. Suddenly, Felipe stood up and started howling. He was crying so hard the tears were shooting out of his eyes. My first thought was that he must have EATEN one of the marshmallows and forgotten to take the toothpick out first.

When I asked him what was wrong, I got no answer, other than the continued impersonation of someone falling down a bottomless pit. I scanned him up and down, and I noticed a toothpick protruding from the side (towards the rear) of his pants. It kind of looked like an Amazon native had shot a blow-dart at him.

I guess the old saying is true – "It's all fun and games until someone gets a toothpick stuck in their ass."

I so badly wanted to ask how the toothpick had gotten there – I mean, after all, they are flimsy little things. I would have thought the toothpick would break or lay flat if sat upon, kind of like a straw can't go through a tree unless driven by hurricane-force winds. But more pressing was the fact that the toothpick was still stuck in his ass. Since Felipe was making no move whatsoever to remove the problem himself, I took it upon myself to pull it out. I was amazed at how hard I had to pull to actually dislodge it.

This was right at the end of class, so I didn't get a chance to find out exactly how the incident had happened. I sent Felipe to the bathroom to clean himself up, and then it was time to go.

Today, we shifted to three-dimensional shapes, and away from toothpicks. I gave each student a net to cut out and paste together to create a geometric solid.

My morning class did pretty well. The only real problem was convincing the kids that their finished product should look like one of the pre-made shapes on my counter, and not like a wadded up Kleenex. Sure, a wadded up Kleenex is, technically, three-dimensional, but that wasn't the point of the lesson.

The afternoon class was much more trying with my already limited patience. Before I could even get the kids started on cutting out the nets, I had to stop several times to review scissor safety and remind the kids that they should NOT clip the shears back and forth in front of their faces. I then had to place not one, but TWO kids in timeout for immediately clipping the shears back and forth in front of their faces.

After the kids had created their figures, I began the unenviable task of coaxing them to explore the attributes. How many faces? What 2-D shapes are the faces? How many edges? How many vertices? No, vertices, not puncture holes from your scissors.

As usual, I had about four kids that were actively participating and trying to answer the questions, while the others did their best showroom window mannequin impersonations.

Finally, the end of the day came around and it was time to dismiss the kids. As I called them to line up, Amir held out something to me. It was the metal tip of his pen, which he had unscrewed.

"Look, this is a cone!" he informed me.

I know I've been losing my patience with this group, and I've been frustrated more often than inspired. However, in that moment right before dismissal, one child demonstrated that he HAD learned something today, and that he could apply that knowledge to a real-world object.

It's always nice to be reassured that SOMETHING is working. And honestly, any day that doesn't end with a kid getting something stuck in his ass should be considered a good day in the history books.

Talk to you later,

Paul E. Hedron

Date: Friday, November 20, 2009
To: Fred Bommerson
From: Jack Woodson
Subject: Whose whine is it anyway?

Hey bud,

I should have known that last email would catch Latya's attention. He always was fascinated by objects being stuck in places they have no business being stuck.

I did ask Felipe the next day what had happened, and he just looked down and whispered, "I sat on it."

I decided not to press the matter. We can only hope it wasn't intentional. After all, sitting on an octagon is one thing, but I have no desire to see anybody purposefully plopping down onto a rectangular pyramid.

Nothing would surprise me, though, because in case I haven't mentioned it, my class this year is extremely immature. I've never had so many kids that still suck their thumbs, display a total lack of listening skills, and repeatedly do the same things over and over and over again, despite being told not to. Case in point, Chassany, who, even after all this time, continues to get in trouble for talking in the hall.

I also notice that many of my kids have a supreme sense of responsibility when it comes to OTHER kids in the room, but they can't seem to look after themselves. They are so worried about the kids around them not following the rules, but they never seem to notice (or care) when they're not following the rules themselves.

I think it's great for kids to take on responsibility, but one of my boys, Lex, always winds up taking responsibility AWAY from somebody else. I'll ask one of the kids to hold open a door so the class can walk through, and seconds later I'll turn around and Lex will be holding the door. Or someone in my class will ask if they can take a basketball out to recess, yet Lex is always the one who winds up holding the ball after lunch.

Mrs. Bird has started calling him "The Sheriff," while I suspect he's been reading his Spiderman comics backwards again and thinks that with great responsibility comes great power.

Yesterday, a few minutes before the bell rang at the end of the day, I asked everyone to clean up the area around their desk, as I always do before we leave the classroom. Usually, it's the kids with the lumber yard right under their desk that ignore me and keep talking, while the kids with a few atoms of dust under their desk are lying prostrate on the floor, trying to make it clean enough to perform open-heart surgery.

As I was asking everyone to look on the floor around them, I looked directly at several scraps of crayon wrapper right underneath Lex's chair. Rather than looking around his own area and picking up the trash, however, Lex noticed that Tyler, on the other side of the room, had a small piece of eraser under his chair. So Lex went running towards Tyler's chair, did a power slide on his knees that would make Tenacious D weep with joy, and picked up the eraser. Then he beamed at me like I was going to award him the Silver Star Award.

And he's only one of many who act this way. Still, the worst of it all is the tattling. I know, I know, I should be used to it by now. After all, tattling in grade school is like the kilt in Scotland – ever present, expected even, but never welcome. Nevertheless, it continues to annoy me.

I think that if teachers didn't receive any base salary at all, but they were given $25 every time one of their students tattled on someone, they could all retire to the Bahamas by the end of the second year.

There is a significant difference between telling the teacher something and telling ON someone. For instance if Tina is hanging upside down from the monkey bars by her shoestrings and can't get down, then yes, that's something I need to know. However, I think I can do without hearing that Billy laughed when Peter dribbled chocolate milk down his chin.

There are many cases when I have to fight mightily to resist the sarcastic response.

Student X:	"Jimmy pointed his middle finger at me!"
Me:	"Really? Then he's not doing it correctly."
Student X:	"He's copying!!"
Me:	"Wow, from YOU? Then he deserves his grade!"
Student X:	"She called my momma fat!"
Me:	"Your momma is not fat. But does she ever Porky Pig?"

Here on board the Tattlestar Galactica, two of my kids take things to the extreme.

I have unofficially given DaQuayvius the cabinet post of Tattle Tale General, since he assaults my ears as soon as he sees me each morning, laying out the entire school population's misdeeds with military precision.

"Sir, status report, Sir! Tommy kicked Lisa's book bag, Kelly was making faces at a second grader, and Donnell is jangling pennies in his pocket. In world news, Lindsay Lohan was busted on DUI charges again."

Then there's Lakeisha, who is constantly tattling about someone or something. And apparently, to anyone who will listen. Today, as her class was entering the cafeteria for lunch, I exited through the other cafeteria door, behind her class, so she was not aware that I was standing there. I actually witnessed her tattle on one of her classmates to some random woman walking down the hall! It was probably some poor second grader's mother, just minding her own business, suddenly accosted by a little girl claiming, "Excuse me, Miss, he just hit me!"

Of course, this lady was able to do what I always wish I COULD do. She kept her eyes straight ahead, didn't make eye contact, and just kept on walking.

Mrs. Frisch told me that she informed her kids at the beginning of the year that she doesn't want to hear any complaining unless it involves one of the 3 B's – Barfing, Bleeding, or Broken. Of course, she has to deal with Roy'al every day, so I think tattling is the least of her worries.

I've overheard Mrs. Bird on more than one occasion tell one of our kids to "Save it for tattle-time." The trick here is that there never IS a tattle-time, but the kids don't seem to catch on to this.

I'm considering creating a tattle patsy. This will be a stuffed animal, or a poster, or even just a stapler – something that I can send the kids to when they really, really have to tell on someone. After all, Lakeisha and others like her just want to speak the words into the air anyway, regardless of who is listening.

I just need to be sure that "Tattle Toby," the stuffed elephant, has eyes that can roll.

Wish me luck on my date with Jill tonight! And please inform Tom Winter that our first date will NOT consist of "going up the hill to fetch a pail of water."

He is so freakin' hilarious.

Later,

Ima Tellonue

Date: Monday, November 30, 2009
To: Fred Bommerson
From: Jack Woodson
Subject: The Nutcracker – Sweet!

Hey man,

How was your Thanksgiving? Can you believe some people don't have turkey as part of their holiday dinner? Jill told me that her family always has chicken on Thanksgiving, and that's just mind-boggling to me. Of course, some people have said that as long as I'm at the table, there will always be a turkey at dinner.

Jill's family lives near San Antonio, so she went down there for most of last week. After our fantastic first date the week before, I'm a little scared of jinxing things by rushing it, but we're on for dinner again this Saturday. In the meantime, I have a few tens of munchkins to attend to.

I liked your suggestion for a tattle spray. Something I could spritz onto a kid that would instantly halt their tattling. Sort of like pepper spray, but with less ocular burning.

I also like how you've already incorporated my "tattle patsy" idea in your own cubicle. For you, it's not so much a "tattle" patsy as it is a "long-winded-droning" patsy. Pretty clever to have a portrait of Jimmy Carter hanging on the file cabinet, so that Darrin will have someone to prattle on and on and on to, while you continue working.

I got an interesting gift today. It's not uncommon for kids to come to school and bring their teachers random little tokens of affection. Usually, it's near one of the major gift-giving holidays like Christmas, or Valentine's Day, or Speak Like a Pirate Day, but it can occur at any time really.

In years past, I have received apples, candy, leaves, drawings, and mugs. Today, I received a nutcracker.

When I say nutcracker, I mean a traditional, wooden, looks-like-a-dude-with-really-scary-dentures nutcracker. Thilleenica brought two to school today – one for me and one for Mrs. Bird. She claims to have one more at home, intended for our principal, Mrs. Forest.

My nutcracker is Scottish, as evidenced by his tartan kilt and big fuzzy hat. So I've given him a Scottish name – Bubba.

Thilleenica says she just likes her teachers so she wanted to give us a gift. I'm touched by her generosity, but it wouldn't surprise me at all if Thilleenica came back tomorrow saying, "Um, turns out I wasn't supposed to give away the family heirlooms."

Bubba won't be leaving my classroom any time soon, just in case. Or at least not until Christmas, when his absence might be discovered.

In the meantime, Bubba can serve as a deterrent to any tomfoolery in the class. If anyone acts up, my immediate statement will be, "Gimme your pinkie! Hold it out!" Believe me, you do NOT want to feel the compressive force of those jaws on your little finger! It's gotta be like 10 PSI!

And if castigation isn't his strong suit, Bubba can always serve as the tattle patsy I've been looking for.

Gifts aside, I was relieved that nobody acted like today was the first day of school, as is sometimes the case after an extended break. We were able to resume where we had left off pretty seamlessly.

Last week was great, though. It's always so nice to have an entire week off from work. The kids were getting a bit crazy, and having some time away from school often settles them down and lets them come back ready to learn again.

This isn't the case for everyone, though. Poor Miss Rooker had to deal with a tiny little lunatic today. This kid is in kindergarten and has been raising holy hell all year long. Today was nuts even by his standards, though. She told me the story at our staff meeting after school today.

Something set the boy off pretty early in the morning, and he started throwing crayons at his classmates. Miss Rooker was called to come take him away and talk to him.

She said that normally, she has a good reputation with this child and that he calms down around her. Today, though, it took a while. In her office, the boy ripped up some papers and broke some pencils on her desk. Then he took off his shoe and threw it at her wall, breaking a picture frame.

She finally got him settled down and talking. Apparently, the kid has a horrible home life with a totally messed up mother. He talked, she listened, he cried, he seemed to be ok.

Later, she took him to lunch, where he had another episode. Something must have offended him greatly. Whether it was the color of the lunch ladies' uniforms or the fact they were serving chicken fingers, we'll probably never know. Whatever it was, the kid started hurling the chicken strips at the ladies, shouting, "FU@% YOU, CAFETERIA PEOPLE!!!"

The way Miss Rooker told it, the kid shouted this invective with the zest of a hard rocker greeting a rabid crowd. "THANK YOU, SAN BERNADINO SCHOOL FOR COWLICK REMOVAL!!"

I wish I could have been there to see the lunch ladies standing behind the counter, dispassionately staring at this kid as the chicken strips bounced harmlessly off the sneeze guard and right back at him.

Apparently, tossing crayons at classmates did not warrant a suspension, but throwing poultry at adults – while cussing – earned him a two-day stay at home.

Not to sound uncaring, but Thursday – the day he returns – is nacho day, and I hope this kid doesn't have any issues with liquid cheese sauce. If he has another incident, I might have to loan out my new nutcracker and make an example out of somebody.
Later,

Chuck N McNuggets

Date:	Friday, December 4, 2009
To:	Fred Bommerson
From:	Jack Woodson
Subject:	3rd grade rocks!

Hey bud,

No, I was only kidding about using the nutcracker as a torture device, so please don't go and call CPS on me. I'm not trying to recreate Goodfellas here. But it HAS been fun having Bubba up on the windowsill at the front of the class.

In the afternoon, when participation is at its lowest, I'll sometimes remark, "I'll bet Bubba knows the answer." Then I entertain myself by counting how many kids actually look at Bubba to see if he'll answer the question.

And yes, the Chicken Finger Whisperer (tell Tiffany, good one!) is indeed a Kindergartener! Must be something in the water supply; they start unraveling early around here.

Lastly, despite what Tom Winter may claim, when I got laid off from Heat Pumps Unlimited, I did NOT mark my exit by shouting, "FU@% YOU, MANUFACTURING PEOPLE!!"

I may have THOUGHT it, but I never vocalized it.

We're touching on a rocky subject here. But that's OK, because for the past couple of weeks, our science topic has been rocks. We have studied igneous, sedimentary, and metamorphic – the Big Three. Since we began, the kids have inundated Mrs. Fitzgerald and me with samples from the playground, their homes, and random gravel quarries. They really want us to see all the different kinds they have found, and they present each one so proudly. Flat rocks, smooth rocks, colored rocks, wood chips, shells, chunks of concrete, hard clumps of dirt, half-eaten candy bars from 1988, and then some.

It's nice of the kids to share their samples with us. My back shelf will soon be full of these rocks and rock-like items. Usually around the time we study leaves at the beginning of the year, my back shelf is filled with different types of leaves that the kids bring in to share with me.

Funny how this phenomenon never happens when we study money.

Speaking of bringing me things, I got another interesting present today. Not to be outdone by Thilleenica and her nutcracker gift, Lakeisha brought me an egg. A no-frills, regular ol' Grade A egg. I was very tempted to put the egg in Bubba's jaws, but I thought that might be seen as a cruel dismissal of Lakeisha's thoughtfulness. Plus, the egg was too big to fit.

Back to our study of rocks, I also talked a bit with the class about volcanoes. Magma and lava are, after all, liquid rock. So today, at around 8:05 (nearly two hours before we do science), Lakeisha motioned me over and said, "I was just going to tell you..." (This is how she begins every statement) "My friend told me that when the world ends, there's going to be lava everywhere, and most people are going to be dead, and the lava is going to kill them."

Of course my smart-alecy mouth couldn't help but respond with, "Really? Lava is going to kill people who are already dead?"

She didn't seem taken aback and instead replied, "No, there's still going to be SOME people who are alive, and the lava is going to kill THEM."

Well then. Good to know.

If I had only been a little quicker on my feet, I could have quizzed Lakeisha with, "And then after the killer lava cools down and solidifies, WHICH type of rock will it be?"

While Lakeisha may be channeling her inner Debbie Downer, another one of my students remains slightly more upbeat. I don't think I've told you about Mia, the little girl who enrolled about a week before Halloween. She's from Mexico, and she doesn't speak much English. She's sweet, but she's also a little goofy. Whenever I give her a little one-on-one assistance, she has an odd way of affirming my help. Instead of a simple, "Thank you," or even, "Gracias," she gets a wide-eyed, almost surprised look on her face, and she shouts, "You a good teacher!" She usually says this loud enough to cause everyone in the room to look up, and she puts emphasis on the word "good."

"You a GOOD teacher!"

So to everyone throughout the years who has thought I was a BAD teacher, I now present the witness for counter-evidence. BOO-YAH!

Miles also gave me props today, in the form of a drawing of Iron Man. Underneath the picture, it said, "Mr.Woodson – a great teacher!" Above the picture was Miles' full name and today's date. I am tempted to add a couple of letters to the drawing and christen this the "Ironic Man" poster, because this is the ONLY time Miles has ever written his name and date on a paper without extensive prompting.

Someone else had names on the brain today as well. Near the end of the day, I was near my door and heard Mrs. Frisch giving a spelling test to one of her kids out in the hallway. She said a word, then used it in a sentence. The student's priority was supposed to be on writing the word down on paper with the correct spelling. What I heard made me sad for the lack of focus AND cracked me up for its spontaneity all at the same time.

Mrs. Frisch:	"The next word is store. Store. John and Tamara went to the store."
Student:	"WHO went?"

Gotta love it. At least she didn't say, "John and Tamara went to the store and were enveloped by lava."

Have a great weekend, man.

Talk to you later,

Val Caynic

Date: Tuesday, December 8, 2009
To: Fred Bommerson
From: Jack Woodson
Subject: The Swine Floozies

Hey Fred,

I beg to differ with you, my friend. I actually WAS referred to as a good worker during my stint at HPU – several times, in fact! Strangely enough, it was often by a Hispanic lady named Mia on the assembly line who would shout, "You a GOOD engineer!"

I'd tell you all about my date over the weekend, except that it never happened. Jill sent me an email late Friday saying that she had to cancel. She would have CALLED to tell me that she had to cancel, but she had completely lost her voice.

Sinusitis, my old nemesis, is now going after my potential loved ones. I've lost my voice a couple of times over the years, and it makes for some REALLY difficult days. I've tried channeling Wiley E Coyote, writing instructions on dry erase boards and holding them up, but the kids look at the board in confusion as if I've written hieroglyphics. I've tried pantomiming instructions, but it was like having the worst teammates ever in a game of charades.

Me: [acting out opening a book and turning pages]
Kids: "Ooooh, I know this one!"
"Throw crayons!"
"Jump up and down on my chair!"
"Punch my neighbor!!"

At any rate, I feel for Jill, but we've been texting back and forth, and she seems to be recovering well. Hopefully, we'll be able to go out this weekend.

I guess it's that cold and illness time of the year, a time when the sniffles get snifflier, the sneezes get frequenter, and the coughs get wetter and hackier. This is the time that justifies the "2 boxes of Kleenex" line on the school supply list.

If I didn't remain vigilant, my kids could easily go through a box of tissues every day. Yesterday, I had to get on to Priya's case for wasting Kleenex. I was already annoyed at her for her over-the-top antics of covering her entire face to impress upon me the fact that she really needed a tissue. But when I saw her grab one tissue, touch it to the tip of her nose, and then immediately grab another tissue, I snapped.

I told her that she owed me a quarter. "Kleenex cost money, you know, so you need to bring a quarter tomorrow for that extra Kleenex you wasted."

By the time Priya came into my class this morning and kept holding out a quarter to me, I had completely forgotten about my little tirade. When she finally told me it was for the Kleenex, I said thank you and took it. Later in the day, I told her that she could have the quarter back if she promised to use only one Kleenex at a time, to which she readily agreed.

I then told her she'd owe me a dollar every time she asked for a Kleenex with both hands covering her face.

I'm thinking I should start charging Tyler a quarter every time I have to listen to one of his health issues. This boy is always complaining about some mysterious malady. As a result, I'm often biting back some snide response to his claims. Or NOT biting them back, in some cases.

A month ago, he told me, "I have a little bump on my head."

Two weeks ago, it was, "My knee kind of hurts."

Last week, I heard, "My eyes are watering."

Often, I just reply with a quick, "Oooh, I'm sorry to hear that."

Other times, I try to express solidarity with the lad by telling him about my own pains.

"I know what you mean, Tyler, my glutes are really tight today!"

Or, "Yeah, my head is pounding like a mo-fo!"

Today, Tyler turned around to tell me, "I have cramps."

I said, "Maybe you're pregnant!"

No, of course I didn't say that. But man, was I tempted!

Tyler's problems pale by comparison to Suzie's. Yes, the same Suzie who falls asleep every single day in class. I don't know if she doesn't sleep at all at home, or if she's doing it for attention, or if nobody's in the hatch of her brain to push the button every 108 minutes to keep her awake.

Yesterday, she left early for a doctor's appointment, and she returned today with a new way to express her problems.

At around 9:00 this morning, she motioned me over so she could tell me, "I'm having girl problems down there." As she said this, she pointed not-so-subtly at her crotch.

Yuck. I'm having regurgitation problems down there, and I'm pointing at my gut.

I don't want to be too cavalier here, because sometimes kids have true health problems. Take Lance and his hemophilia, for instance. But I feel like Tyler, Suzie, and the others will need to suffer a massive heart attack, a stroke, and a really nasty hangnail (what we in the medical industry term "The Trifecta") before I really start worrying about them.

Well, my angina and sciatica are starting to act up, and I think I feel a touch of e. coli coming on. I had better wrap this up! Talk to you later,

Hy Pocondriak

Date:	Friday, December 11, 2009
To:	Fred Bommerson
From:	Jack Woodson
Subject:	Joaqim Possible and the Scorched Earth

Hey pal,

From what you're telling me, it sounds like Steph in HR has gotten even worse since I left Heat Pumps Unlimited. It's one thing to have kids like Tyler and Suzie constantly complaining about how they feel, but it's much worse coming from an adult. Steph is STILL talking about catching Swine Flu? Wasn't that like two years ago?

A word of advice – don't mention lice to her, or she'll suddenly have it and need to go home immediately.

I am so glad that today is Friday. Besides having a date tonight with a fully recovered Jill (YES!), my carpal tunnel syndrome has really been aggravating me. You may remember, that was one of my wonderful parting gifts for years of service at HPU (along with a lovely assortment of salted meats and a year's supply of Rice-a-Roni, the San Francisco Treat). It had gone away for a while, but it's been making a resurgence lately. Today, my hands felt weaker than Carson Daly's charisma.

For the past two days, I've been wearing one of those wrist braces – you know, the kind that makes it looks like I'm going on the professional bowling tour. Of course the kids keep asking me, "Mister Woodson, what happened to your hand?"

I tell them, "I've just always wanted to be a super hero!"

Now I shall be known as Mister Iron Fist. Well, I guess I'm really more like Mister Rigid Plastic and Polymer Blend (with Delicate Weave!) Fist. To everyone except Shelly, that is, who still insists on calling me "Miss."

While ruling the class with my cyborg fist, I've been attempting to teach elapsed temperature problems. That's right, ELAPSED temperature problems. When I was in school, I'm pretty sure we never did anything like this, certainly not in the third grade. In fact, I don't even think I heard the word "elapsed" until after I had my master's degree in engineering! But anyway, it's on the curriculum, so it must be taught. The problems are all of this sort:

"This morning, the temperature outside was 74°F. By the afternoon, it had risen to 88°F. What was the change in temperature?"

After seeing this on the test my very first year and realizing what difficulty my kids were having with it, I started practicing the skill with subsequent classes much earlier in the year. Most of the kids this year have gotten pretty good at it, but a few of them always want to add the numbers, regardless of how high they are or what they mean.

Yes, Unthinking One, the temperature went up 162 degrees today! Let's not stop to consider whether or not that makes any sense, let's just add numbers, because adding is fun! WHEEEEE!! Who wants sugar??

Whenever I see a kid who has chosen such an answer, I always ask him, "Do you realize how hot that is? If the temperature ever went up that much, we would all die! There would be fires! Earthquakes!! Dogs and cats living together!!! MASS HYSTERIA!!!!"

Sadly, they never seem to take the hint (or recognize the movie quote).

Ironically, Lakeisha – harbinger of the fiery apocalypse – always gets these elapsed temperature problems correct.

I guess I shouldn't be too surprised that they have such difficulty with this, because their internal body thermostats are quite clearly on the fritz. Every August, when it's over 100 degrees outside, there are kids running around the playground wearing big bulky sweatshirts. And every winter when it's freezing, there are kids who come to school in shorts.

I am encouraged, though, that all of the kids DO understand another concept we've been discussing – probability. At the end of the day, as I was getting ready to draw some tickets for the prize basket, I thought I'd test the kids' understanding. At the third grade level, probability is not daunting at all. It boils down to one of four options. Something is either most likely, least likely, equally likely, or impossible. If there are 3 red blocks, 3 green blocks, 1 blue block, and 6 yellow blocks in a box, then yellow is most likely to be picked, blue is least likely, red and green are equally likely, and mauve with polka-dots is impossible.

You know I give out blue tickets to the kids for good behavior and participation. They then put their names on the tickets, and I draw three tickets on Friday for prizes. As I stirred the tickets around in the bowl today and all eyes were upon me, I asked, "Who would be IMPOSSIBLE for me to pick right now?"

I was expecting answers like, "Mrs. Bird!" or, "President Obama!" or even, "Fred Bommerson!"

Instead, nearly every single kid shouted, "JOAQIM!!"

I was momentarily taken aback, but as I glanced at Joaqim, slouched in his chair, he shrugged sheepishly and said, "Yeah, I don't have any tickets in there."

You know what this means? They get it!! They all totally understand probability – or at least what the term "impossible" means! Even perennial underperformer Joaqim, who is hard pressed to understand how a crayon works!

Success!

Now if I can just get those few kids to realize that it is IM-POSSIBLE for the temperature to rise over 150 degrees in one day. Except of course for that day when lava covers the earth and kills all of the dead people.

Talk to you later,

Sir Tenn

Date: Tuesday, December 15, 2009
To: Fred Bommerson
From: Jack Woodson
Subject: Clear and present manger

Hey bud,

I had another great date with Jill. There is definitely something special there, and it's not just our shared disdain for standardized tests and empty mechanical pencils. I told her about Joaqim and his improbable breakthrough, and she thought it was funny, though she didn't start naming kids that are most likely, least likely, and impossible to pass, as you did. And tell Winter to stop saying my class has jumped the shark. This isn't a TV show, you know!

Here at school, it's beginning to look a lot like Christmas. Excuse me, I should say it's beginning to look a lot like Holiday Season. I've never particularly been one for euphemisms (despite the cruel joke my parents played on me by giving me the middle name "Euphemism"), and that one especially chaps my hide. Why isn't February the "Holiday Season?" I mean, you've got Valentine's Day, Presidents' Day, Groundhog Day, MY birthday... talk about a holiday bonanza!

But no, we can't officially talk about Christmas in school anymore – Heaven forbid! (Wait, can I say the word "Heaven?") During the morning announcements today, Mrs. Forest capped things off with, "Remember, kids, there are only four school days left until Chris – Winter Break!"

I could practically hear her larynx split down the middle as it attempted to do a 180 and avoid saying the C-word.

Call me a rebel, but I haven't corrected any of my kids who have mentioned "Christmas Break" in class. I haven't refrained from using those words myself. And I sure as heck haven't removed Bubba, the Christmas-Specific Nutcracker.

This crazy weather we're having seems to have given some kids a reason to start Christmas vacation early! Last night, when I got home, it was almost 80° outside. Today after school, I threw a couple of snowballs at the buses as they left.

Yes, the temperature dropped that far in less than 24 hours. Please entirely disregard my previous email about elapsed temperature impossibilities. While it didn't start snowing until around 11 o'clock, it was 34° on my drive in to the school. And for that half an hour that I had to stand out in front of the school on crosswalk duty, it didn't get any warmer. I had on my ski cap, gloves, and scarf, and I was still miserable. My crosswalk partner, Mr. Vann, was bundled up like a Tusken Raider – with better conversational skills, of course. We didn't greet nearly as many kids as usual, because a lot of parents must have watched the weather reports, seen what was coming, and kept their children at home.

After the morning announcements had ended and after I had regained feeling in my extremities, Mrs. Forest came on the speaker again and asked for a head count so that the cafeteria would know how many lunches to have ready. I sent a few kids out to collect up numbers from the other third grade teachers, and the results came back looking like Mike Vanderjagt's field-goal record as a Dallas cowboy. 10/17, 14/17, 16/21, etc.

I had just 3 kids missing out of 18, but Mrs. Bird only had 11 out of her 17 present. So in the afternoon, after we had switched classes – and after two parents had come to pick up their children – I had a ridiculously small class. It was actually quite pleasant.

Lex and Tyler had caused a lot of trouble yesterday for the substitute teacher while I was at a training. So today, I had both of them sitting at their seats repeatedly copying the phrase, "I will not misbehave and act like a fool."

I can only hope that one day that message will stick!

At 2:00, Cerulean and Felipe went to their resource class, and Ella was picked up by her mother. I started to feel like I was stuck in an Agatha Christie novel – And Then There Were Six.

I'm pretty sure this is the first time in my teaching career that I have had less than ten kids at the end of the day. Even on the last day of school, I've never had this few.

It will be very interesting to see how tomorrow goes. The forecast calls for highs in the mid-40s, and as far as I know, there are no plans to close the schools. However, it is supposed to be in the 20s tomorrow MORNING, and seeing as how that is when parents decide whether or not to send their kids out the door, I would not be surprised to have only a handful of kids again. Unfortunately, I can almost guarantee that the misbehaving fools will be first in line at my doorway. In shorts.
Talk to you later,

Shelby Freezing

Date:	Thursday, December 17, 2009
To:	Fred Bommerson
From:	Jack Woodson
Subject:	It's 3:00 PM. Do you know where your parents are?

Hey man,

I had wondered if the attendance there at the plant might be similar to the attendance I was seeing at school. Especially for people like Mary Pickens or Les Johnson. They practically live in Oklahoma! I wouldn't want their commute on a NORMAL day!

It doesn't surprise me at all that Larry would take both days off and then call everyone repeatedly to let them know he was industriously working from home.

My numbers yesterday were slightly lower than what I had told you about on Tuesday. I let the kids play math games for most of the day, and it gave me a chance to do a little individual work with a few of the lower kids like Cerulean, who was cheating on the math games anyway.

Today, with the temperatures back up above freezing, my classes were once again at full capacity.

It's hard to believe, but tomorrow is the last school day of 2009! It's the last work day of the year for you, too! It should be a super-easy, fun, party day. Well, for me, I mean. EVERY day is like that for YOU, right?

Mrs. Bird and I are planning on having very short class periods and then putting both groups together for the party. I don't have a whole lot planned academically. The kids need to take their multiplication test – it's the 5's, so there SHOULD be no problems – and we have a little bit of science to finish up.

After lunch, we're going to show Toy Story 2. If anybody questions the "academic merit" of showing such a film, I will readily expound on how we have been talking about non-renewable resources, such as oil, which is used to make plastic, which we are observing in the forms of Woody and Buzz.

Like I said, tomorrow should be a fun day. Today, on the other hand, was a long day, complete with a cafeteria malfunction that brought about sack lunches and necessitated that teachers eat with their kids. I found myself wedged in between Gwenn and Ava, being bombarded with questions like, "Are you Team Edward or Team Jacob?"

I thought my answer – Team Spiderman – should have been fairly obvious.

Near the end of the lunch period, Miles said he didn't like chocolate pudding and offered me his. I graciously accepted. Then Priya offered me hers. Then Smoker Anna. Before I knew it, I had a pudding pyramid in front of me.

I left the cafeteria with a sack containing fifteen cups of chocolate pudding. So you're probably thinking, "Man, I know what HE'LL be doing over Christmas break!"

Today also presented me with several of the most interesting interactions with parents I've ever had, outside of Conference Night. Jacob Marley warned Scrooge that he would be visited by three ghosts. Nobody informed ME that I would make contact with three parents before this day was through.

The first came in the form of an email during my planning period. When we met with Victor's mom one day after school last month, she gave us her email address and asked us to use it if Victor was not doing his homework or took any more trips to the planet Zorlon. I've emailed her several times since then, though it hasn't seemed to have had a whole lot of impact on his work ethic.

Today, I received an email from Victor's mother with the subject line "FWD: Ninja Kitties." I had been cc'ed, along with twelve other people, and the only thing the email contained was a movie file.

Granted, the video clip WAS hilarious. I mean, who wouldn't enjoy seeing a cat leap out of nowhere and attach itself to some dude's crotch? But what I don't get is what on earth would possess this lady to think that I want to be part of her email forwarding group?? Am I now going to start receiving jokes of the day, top ten lists, and chain messages from Bill Gates? Is she going to friend request me on Facebook?

The second parent contact came after school. I had completely forgotten about the weird thumping sound that my car started to make as I pulled into the parking lot this morning. At the time, I had pulled into the nearest parking spot and looked under my front tires VERY quickly. It was super cold and still pretty dark. It looked like a little piece of plastic had come loose and was bumping against the tire. I didn't think about it again all day long.

At around 4:30, when I started to pull out of the parking space, my memory was jolted, and I immediately knew I had a flat tire. What I had failed to notice this morning was a piece of metal wire about two feet long and about a quarter inch in diameter sticking out of my tire.

After the customary amount of cursing had been purged from my system, I broke out the jack and spare tire from my trunk and started to take the lug nuts off.

Not too long after, I heard a voice say, "Do you need some help?"

I looked up to see Vito's father standing there. You may remember Vito from my class last year. His family lives in the neighborhood, and the parents walk the kids to school every day. They also walk back up to the school every evening to play on the playground. The kids play, not the parents.

I stood up to say hi to Vito's father, and almost immediately, he practically shoved me out of the way to complete changing the tire. Honestly, I did very little but watch and roll the spare over to him.

Afterwards, when I shook his hand and thanked him profusely, he simply said, "No problem. You taught my son last year."

Wow, I guess there ARE some tangible rewards to being a teacher after all!

After a not so quick stop at the tire store, I drove to the nearby Super Target. Tomorrow night, Mrs. Caring is having a Holiday – no! Christmas! – party at her house, and I stopped to get some adult beverages and chips.

I didn't need to spend long in the store, having just a couple of things to grab. I took my items up to the cash register, said hi to the cashier, put my items on the conveyor belt, and started flipping through my wallet. As I was pulling out the ol' magic plastic money card, the cashier asked, "So how is my daughter doing?"

I completely had not recognized Ella's mother, who was standing behind the counter and waiting for me to reply. She hadn't worn the Target apron to parent conference night, and that must have thrown me off.

I tried to recover as best I could. "She's doing pretty well, actually. She seems to be paying more attention in class – oh, could you put the booze in a separate bag, please? – though she has turned in a few incomplete homeworks."

While we waited for the credit card transaction to go through, I considered asking her if she had seen the ninja kitties video on the internet, but I figured I had already embarrassed myself enough by not recognizing her.

I really need to remember not to do my shopping so close to the school.

Well hey, have fun at the HPU Christmas party! Be sure to take pictures or video if Larry once again transforms into "Ted, the guy who hangs mistletoe in inappropriate places."
Merry Christmas!

Gene E Awlogee

Date: Wednesday, January 6, 2010
To: Fred Bommerson
From: Jack Woodson
Subject: Don't I know you?

Hey bud,

I haven't heard from you since the New Year's Eve party at Winter's place, so I hope you've managed to recover fully. I guess you realize now that you're too old to do tequila shots, and even more importantly, GIN shots are a horrible idea at ANY age.

Have you made any New Year's resolutions? Here are a few of mine:

Continue to teach our society's youth the basics and complexities of mathematics – after all, they are our future.

Establish a space base on faraway Pluto. It might not be recognized as a planet anymore, but it still has strategic value.

Learn a new language. I'm waffling between Elvish and Na'vi.

Further explore my newfound love for the cranberry.

Display compassion and patience with the students placed in my care, and stop snapping them with rubber bands.

Yesterday was the kids' first day back after Christmas vacation. As expected, there was a lot of information that had been forgotten over the break, many groggy expressions, and a great disdain for having to be back at the school again. But enough about MY attitude; the kids were pretty good.

Before we left for break, several children gave me little gifts. I got some decorative candy containers, a candle or two, a tranquility fountain, and a couple of other items. So today, I handed out thank you cards to those kids who had begifted me. As a stocking stuffer, my mom gave me a set of Justice League thank you notes. Superman, Batman, the Flash, et al. graced the front side, and my heartfelt appreciation graced the inside.

Reactions were mixed. Jacob actually seemed embarrassed to be receiving a superhero card from his teacher, while Tomas exclaimed, "I'm too old for Batman!"

To which I replied, "Well I'm not!"

Clearly, I am going to have to go in tomorrow wearing my Batman tie, my green power ring, and maybe even a red cape for good measure. But not my Incredible Hulk underoos. He's not in the Justice League, and the underoos are in the wash.

While I didn't lose any students over the break, I did gain two new ones yesterday. Ta'varon and Demontrae are brothers, but not twins. That's never a good portent for the older one, in this case, Demontrae.

Ta'varon is in my homeroom and Demontrae went to Mrs. Bird. Already, I can see tiny little differences, like the fact that Ta'varon is friendly and easy-going, while Demontrae is surly and workophobic.

Happy New Year to me!

While I was getting my new student settled, Mrs. Frisch came into my room and caused a bit of embarrassment. I can't remember if you've ever met her or not, but you'd never forget her if you had. I love her to death, but the woman has no volume control.

She walked in right after announcements and said, "Hey, Jack. Did you have a nice break? How are things going with your new girlfriend? Are you in LUUUUUUVVV?"

This was in her normal tone of voice, which is only slightly quieter than a jet engine.

Naturally, all of the kids had stopped any pretense of doing their work and were just staring at me. I almost expected Jessie or Smoker Anna to ask, "Yeah, Jack, how IS your new relationship?"

I awkwardly told Mrs. Frisch I would talk to her later and drove our visitor out of the room.

This afternoon, though, I had a fantastic surprise visitor that was also a blast from the past. Pinar, one of my favorite students from my very first year of teaching (actually, one of my all-time favorites) stopped by my classroom around 2:00 today. She's in the tenth (!!!!) grade in a nearby district, and they don't go back to school until next week.

I was right in the middle of working a word problem with the kids when she came in, so after the exclamations and hugs, I told the kids that we had a guest teacher, and I let her take over for me. My kids from this year seemed absolutely flabbergasted that standing before them was an actual, real life example of someone who had been in my class years ago. They were practically falling over themselves trying to get Pinar to call on them as she went through the steps of the problem.

When she was done, she informed me, "I don't really like math."

D'OH!!!

We chatted for a few minutes, and I learned that she had skipped 5th grade, she was on her school's volleyball team, and she still thought fondly of her old teachers. She was disappointed that Mrs. Swanson wasn't at the school anymore but seemed very happy to hear about her two kids. We exchanged email addresses, and then she left to look for Miss Rooker.

Seeing Pinar made me think back on some of my other kids from my rookie year. I wonder if Kelvin is still rapping and dancing, if Ariel is still so overly somber, and if Marvin is still telling everybody that he tastes like chicken.

I'll bet none of THOSE kids are too old for Batman.

Talk to you later,

The Flashback

Date:	Tuesday, January 12, 2010
To:	Fred Bommerson
From:	Jack Woodson
Subject:	Full court mess

Hey buddy,

Yes, I know full well that YOU are not too old for superheroes, but I'm not in the practice of writing thank you cards to people for dating advice. BAD advice, at that! Jill would most definitely NOT be impressed if I showed up wearing jean shorts, flip flops, and three popped collars.

Speaking of flip flops, I'm surprised you remember Esteban from my first year. I doubt that he skipped a grade like Pinar did, so that would make him a high school freshman this year. I wonder if he'd tell me the name of his girlfriend.

"AMANDA!"

"NO, CHRISTY!!"

"WAIT, IT'S KIMBERLY!!!"

Today we started something that wasn't done during my first year at all. It's an "enrichment" program after school on Tuesdays. (Sounds like something to do with wheat and associated by-products, right?) From 3:15-4:30, most of the teachers stay and supervise a group of kids in a specific activity. Some teachers run a soccer club, some do cheerleading, some do puzzles and Legos, some do chess. I wanted to do a "Texas Two-Card Hold 'Em" club, but they wouldn't let me. I don't know why not, it would reinforce mathematical concepts of probability and multiplication. Instead, I chose to lead a basketball club.

I had a group of seventeen third graders (not just my own) at the outdoor baskets today, and the first thing I did was teach them how to play Knock Out. This is a fast-moving game involving two basketballs and a fair share of coordination. I'm holding off on teaching them anything that requires TOO much coordination, like the full court three-man weave or the 360 Tomahawk dunk. We'll save that for the advanced club.

We were having a lot of fun, and the atmosphere was very relaxed. At one point, when several kids had hit consecutive baskets, I shouted, "I'm gonna start calling you 'butter,' cuz you're on a roll!" This brought on a stunned, "HUH???" from several kids, and it effectively ended the streak. Note to self: third graders not yet ready for SportsCenter.

They did have their own little catch phrase, though. Whenever somebody made a shot – and quite often even when somebody just TOOK a shot – several of the boys would yell, "SWAGGER!"

I'm not familiar with this interjection at all, and nobody could tell me what it meant or why they were saying it, other than that they had heard other people say it. Even Tyler, who was screaming it the loudest and most aggressively, had no idea WHY he was screaming it.

This made me want to see if I could get them to say something else nonsensical.

The next time I made a shot, I shouted, "PICANTE!"

That got me some strange looks. I told the kids, "That's what we used to say back in the day."

I continued to shout it every time I made a shot. As I had hoped, by the end of the day, a couple of boys had tentatively shouted, "Khan-tay!" after making a basket.

As I was playing with the kids, it made me think back on some of my fond basketball memories. Going winless in my senior year of high school was not one of them. Being compared to a spider monkey by the Guam Bomb didn't make the list either. But one of my brother's 8th grade games IS up there as a high point.

My dad was the coach of Zack's team, and I helped out as an assistant coach. This particular game was against the dreaded arch-rival, so we enacted Operation: Super Spazz. The Saturday morning of the game, I dressed as one of the team. I was a senior in high school, so I was already at full-size – 6'4", 180 lbs – and I stood out monstrously from the other kids on the court. In addition to my size advantage, I had meticulously cultivated a wild, animalistic appearance. I wore a pair of racquetball-style goggles (think Kareem Abdul-Jabbar, circa mid-80s) and the most severe case of bedhead this side of Jimmy Fallon.

During pre-game warm-ups, I participated in the layup lines, each time running full speed at the basket and heaving the ball at the backboard as hard as possible. I was going for maximum rebound distance, hoping to have to chase the ball past half court into the opposing ranks. With each heave, I let out a primal yell, like the Goonies' Sloth trying to free himself from imprisonment. I think at one point, I even picked up one of my brother's teammates and shook him around.

Once the game started, I couldn't play of course, so I sat on the bench. But the psychological impact was visible. The other team's point guard frequently stole glances over at our bench, and whenever he did, I pointed at him and made a gesture like Ozzy Osbourne biting the head off of a bat. They played scared the entire game, and we won easily. Years later, in high school, my brother became buddies with several of the players from that team, and one of them confided in him that he had almost wet his pants that day.

Making memories. That's what I'm all about.

Talk to you later,

Arlen Globetrotter

Hey dude,

I apologize for giving you such a sports overloaded email earlier this week. I sometimes forget what a sports weenie you are, and that even athletes' nicknames tend to confuse you. Though it's certainly entertaining for the rest of us when you talk about Michael "The Refrigerator" Jordan, Alex "Air" Rodriguez, and Wayne "Too Tall" Gretzky.

But let's move away from sports.

Earlier this week, Miss Gellar, a special ed teacher, approached me in the hall and asked if I had a boy named Maurice in my class. She told me that she thought he might be responsible for some graffiti out on the playground, as some writing with his name on it had been found on the inside of one of the tube slides.

I told her that none of my kids ever write their names on anything, so it was probably the Maurice in Mrs. Fitzgerald's class. I did ask what he had written, though. I was fully expecting to hear that he had spelled "F-U-K" or "B-I-C-H-T." Instead, Miss Gellar said the graffiti read, "Maurice has 25 hot wheels cars. His friend has 19 hot wheels cars. How many cars in all?"

Maurice is a math graffiti artist! SCORE!! Just kidding, nobody should be defacing school property. But hey, if you've got to write something onto the side of a public façade, why not make it something that is likely to stimulate brain cells?

Since we've been back from vacation, we've been focusing pretty hard on word problems. Maurice's example notwithstanding, this has proven to have many "problems" of its own.

Most word problems follow some sort of logical path. Most third graders do not. So while it might make perfect sense to you or me that if somebody gives away five pencils, they should then have LESS pencils than they started with – prompting subtraction – that's not always the way it works out.

Usually, when we walk through a problem together out loud in a class discussion, logic prevails. The kids, even the low ones, can tell me when they should add and when they should subtract. The problem arises when the kids face the questions on their own.

The main issue being that many of the kids don't actually read the problem or think about what the words mean.

Did you ever see that Far Side cartoon captioned, "What dogs hear?" The human says, "Spot, fetch my slippers! Good boy, Spot, that's a good boy, Spot!" and the dog hears, "Spot, blah blah blah blah blah, Spot, blah blah blah blah Spot!"

Gary Larson could do a similar cartoon called, "What kids read."

"Blah blah blah blah blah blah 15 blah blah. Blah blah blah blah blah blah 3 blah blah. Blah blah blah blah blah?"

The kid would then go through a complicated thought process – "Ooooooh, I spy, with my tiny little eye, two numbers!! The magic 8-ball in my head says to ADD them! Adding is my favorite!"

Then the teacher, ME, reads their answer and wonders why the heck each friend has 18 hotdogs, if Alex started with 15 hotdogs and split them up evenly among 3 friends. (Never mind the fact that they added hotdogs and friends and magically turned them all into hotdogs.)

Anyway, Mrs. Fitzgerald, Miss Palmerstein, and I had a brilliant idea last week. We figured that a great way to help the kids get even better with math problems AND to save ourselves the effort of searching through books for good homework was to have the kids do ALL of the work. So their "test" today was to write their own word problems. They were allowed to write as many as they wanted, but they had to write at least one problem that required addition and at least one problem that required subtraction.

Some of the problems that I received were actually quite well written, and some were endearingly hilarious. It was clear that nearly all of the kids put their best effort forward.

Here are some of the standouts:

"Felipe has 24 suckers and he gave Tyler 10 of them. How many suckers did he have left?"
This might not seem so special, but it came from Felipe, one of my absolute lowest students.

"On Friday, I had a test of addition and there were 12 problems. I only finished 5 of them. How many more did I need to do?"

A fantastic subtraction problem from Thilleenica that doesn't involve anything being given or taken away.

"Antonio and Victor went to school. Antonio did the Pledge of Allegiance 20 times. The next day, Victor did the Pledge of Allegiance 50 times. How many times did they do it all together?"
I'm telling you, I make them recite it until they get it right, and there are no more mentions of "One Asian, under God."

"Ta'varon had 5 sisters. 2 of them went to college. How many sisters does he have now?"
Well, still five, I think. Unless of course they went to North Carolina, in which case it would stand to reason that they are dead to him.

"Yesterday, the temperature was 34° F. What will be the change in temperature during the night?"
Eddie posed a question more suited for our meteorologists than our third graders.

"Mister Woodson has 99 markers. He received 900 more markers. Mister Woodson has a nice haircut. How many markers does Mister Woodson have in all?"
An interesting choice of random extra information, and Tyler's nose WAS a bit browner than usual today.

And finally, a question from Cerulean, who unfortunately just doesn't understand the concept.
"Derrick had $22 in the bank. He spent $32 for his lunch. How many more money does he have left?"
I hope this poor girl doesn't get her hands on a credit card anytime soon, because I'm afraid she's going to be upside-down immediately.

I'm going to take several of the good ones and use them as morning problems and homework problems next week. And if one or two of them show up on the swing set or monkey bars, I will disavow any knowledge of said problems.
Later,

Saul V Kwaytion

Date: Thursday, January 21, 2010
To: Fred Bommerson
From: Jack Woodson
Subject: I have a bean!

Hey bud,

I wouldn't expect for you to see any third grade word problems scrawled on the walls there at the factory. Ben Marston from R&D HAS been known to scribble chemical formulas on the bathroom stall door, though, so watch out for that. He claimed that inspiration struck at an awkward moment when he didn't have anything to write on. Us dumb jock guys pointed out that he was sitting right next to an entire roll of writing material, and he seemed stunned. You know those brainiac guys – can't see the toilet paper for the trees.

By the way, I forgot to mention it last time, but I REALLY wish I could have seen the look on Larry's face when you shouted, "PICANTE!" over his cubicle wall. I just think you shouldn't have explained it to him. You should have left him wondering what the heck you were smoking.

I hope you're having a great week. I myself am having a very short week. We had Monday off for MLK Day, and Tuesday was our semester transition teacher work day. One semester down and one to go! We've made it through 1/2 of the year, we've got 2/3 left to go, and only 12/9 of my kids understand fractions.

It's amazing how the short weeks always feel like the longest. I think the kids feel like they have to cram a week's worth of foolishness into a mere three days.

In honor of the holiday, Mrs. Bird had her kids reading and writing about Martin Luther King, Jr. She gave them mini-biographies and asked them to make a "biography quilt" on a large piece of construction paper.

She brought one of the quilts and one of the books over to show me. First, she asked me to read a page in the book that said Dr. King hoped to inspire Americans "through his peaceful efforts."

Then she showed me the quilt where Temperance had mis-copied this sentiment as, "through his space full of farts."

Ironically enough, this lets me segue smoothly into my next topic – gas. Well, also solids and liquids. We studied the three states of matter last week, and over the long weekend, I gave the kids a homework assignment where they had to make a list of items around their homes that fell into these three categories.

As I expected, I got some interesting responses in terms of our three states of matter. It's always fun to read these lists and see what unique items the kids put on their lists. I'm sad to say that so far in my teaching career, no one has listed Nightcrawler's smelly BAMF cloud or Terminator 2's liquid metal.

I'm always curious to see which kids are daring/reckless enough to put any bodily functions on their list. Last year, one boy did list "fart" under the gas column. Good for him for thinking outside the box. Just so long as he keeps things inside the bowl.

This year, nobody expressed any kind of flatulence, though Miles did list a bunch of solid foods in the "gas" column that would make anyone toot. Baked beans, baked rice, baked everything.

Jacob and Tomas put ketchup on their lists of liquids, so as you might expect, I immediately gave them both a grade of 500. And before you even reply, Fred, I don't need to hear a lecture about thixotropic solids and whatnot; from a 3rd grader, I will accept ketchup as a liquid.

The most entertaining entry came from Clarisa, whose list of liquids revealed a lot about her home life. First there was Bud Light. Then came Clamato. Naturally, the list ended with Pepto Bismol.

Not turning in a list were my two newest cast members in this two-act play I call third grade. They're part-time players, anyway. These two are from the Behavioral Unit.

At our school, we have a handful of kids who are, for whatever reason, deemed unable to function in a regular classroom environment. Don't ask me how they select the kids for this unit, because I can't for the life of me understand how Roy'al is not among them.

Patrick and Felicia are kids that are being slowly reintegrated into the mainstream system. They are only with me for science class every day, and a teacher from the Behavioral Unit is supposed to be with them in class at all times.

Patrick has been at this school for a while, so I'm already somewhat familiar with him. He's an Eddie Haskell type. If he thinks you're not watching him, he'll punch another kid or spit on someone. Then when you look at him, he'll put on a huge smile and tell you how he loves your tie and your choice of footwear.

Felicia is new to the school. Ms. Hamm, the special ed teacher, told me a little about her last week when they knew she was transferring. Ms. Hamm told me that Felicia seems sweet enough, but that she has frequent anxiety attacks. Oh, and she sees monsters. So she has to carry around a spray bottle of pepper water – I'm assuming that this is exactly what it sounds like – to ward off these monsters.

My first question to Ms. Hamm was, "Can I spray pepper water at some of MY monsters, like Lex and Demontrae?"

Yesterday, Patrick and Felicia didn't come to my class. Apparently, they weren't ready. Today, Ms. Whitney accompanied them, and they sat at a table in the back. Ms. Whitney mostly watched over the two Behavioral Unit kids, but she wasn't hesitant to help out with a few other kids as well. When I asked the kids to take out their science books, Ms. Whitney noticed that Eddie hadn't complied. She shouted at him, "He SAID, take out your book!!" and he immediately did.

Something tells me that SHE won't have to play Simon Says with him. In fact, when she yelled at him, I'm pretty sure he let a little bit of all three states of matter out of his body.

Might want to check your shorts for cake, kid.

Talk to you later,

Saul Idstate

Date: Tuesday, January 26, 2010
To: Fred Bommerson
From: Jack Woodson
Subject: Code Clown on Aisle 9!

Hey man,

I think that the only way you're ever truly going to be rid of your problem is if you sit down and write a formal letter to Paul and/or Reggie, stating that you neither need nor want an example-filled lesson on the three states of matter every time you visit Larry's cubicle. Be sure to mention that you have it on good authority that the phrase "Pull my finger" is not how most teachers introduce the gas phase.

Beware, though; if Larry counters your complaint by saying, "It's for science!" your case goes out the window.

I haven't actually gotten to see Felicia's pepper water yet, so I can't answer your question about the delivery system. I would guess it's just a recycled Windex bottle or something. I've also refrained from asking her about the monsters. As it so happens, she's not the only third grader with monsters on her mind.

Yesterday, as we were coming back inside from recess, several of my girls were enthusiastically telling me that somebody had seen a clown outside, and that this clown had killed a kid. Our transitional conversation usually isn't quite so morbid. Most of the time, it ranges from, "Mr. Woodson, I forgot my jacket!" to, "Mr. Woodson, I forgot my sweater!" with the occasional, "Mr. Woodson, I left my book outside!" thrown in for good measure.

I pretty much ignored the killer clown comments, instead reminding the kids to "be ninjas" as we walked down the hallway. That's my code phrase for, "Knock off all that jibber jabber!"

The phenomenon would not be ignored for long, however.

Today at recess, before any of the teachers realized what was going on, a huge group of third graders (about 50 or 60) had gathered out in the far corner of the soccer field where there is a sewer grate. I had a feeling they weren't holding a poetry slam, so I went out to the field and chased them all back onto the playground, only to hear about twenty confirmations that there was indeed a killer clown living down in the sewer.

Well, this clinches it. Someone has been watching Stephen King's "It." Ten years ago, I would have bet good money that no eight-year-old ever would have been allowed to watch a scary movie like that, but my first year of teaching quelled those thoughts. Now I know it's not at all uncommon for these kids to watch High School Musical and Freddy vs. Jason in the same weekend.

Not only that, but I also have firsthand proof that my kids are so brilliant that instead of running FROM a would-be homicidal circus freak, they would actually swarm CLOSER to it. Have I mentioned that I do NOT work at a Vanguard school?

Most of the kids seem (I hope!) to know that it's just a big gag. But Ella seems genuinely terrified. While the other kids were trying to top each other's gruesome stories about the clown, I noticed Ella wincing in terror, as if the Statue of Liberty's head had just gone careening past her. Miss Rooker had to take her out of class this afternoon and talk with her about it, trying to calm her fears.

I can only hope that next week, nobody comes to school talking about a red and white 1958 Plymouth Fury that can drive itself.

Later in the day, there was another terrifying incident. I don't know if it was from fear of Pennywise the Killer Clown or from a bad reaction to the fish sticks, but Hillary couldn't keep her lunch down.

Around 1:30, I was stooped down by Tyler's desk, helping him with a math problem. All of a sudden, from the other side of the room, I heard the sound of 500 wet paper clips hitting the floor. Ah yes, someone had blown chunks.

I stood up and saw Hillary staring at me with a stained shirt and glazed eyes. She looked like she was in a trance, just waiting to be told what to do. Had I shouted, "VOMIT!" she probably would have puked again. Had I screamed, "JUGGLE BOWLING PINS!!" she might have attempted it. Instead, I shouted, "GO TO THE BATHROOM!!"

Meanwhile, every other eyeball in the room was riveted to the suspiciously Oreo-colored puddle on the floor. My sarcastic inner voice came out, and I couldn't help saying, "PLEASE! Keep staring at the throw up! Let's all get a REALLY good look at the vomit and make ourselves sick! Tomorrow, be sure to bring a camera, so you can take a picture!"

WHY??? Why do these kids STARE at throw up? Personally, MY reaction to someone vomiting is to get as far away as possible from that person and their hurlage. Not these kids, though.

Oooh, somebody got sick and made a disgusting mess? Let's stick our noses in it and get the full sensory experience!

Wow, there's a murderous clown running around? Let's go see if we can find it and catch its attention! Those toothpicks might be dangerously sharp? Let's see how many we can get stuck in our butt cheeks!

Well buddy, I'm going to let you go now. I think I've got some milk in the fridge that expired in December, so I'm going to see how it smells and tastes.

Later,

Pepe La Puke

Date: Friday, January 29, 2010
To: Fred Bommerson
From: Jack Woodson
Subject: There will be flood

Hey man,

No, I never did discover who actually started the Killer Clown rumor. Chassany tried to tell me one day, but all I heard was, "I heard it from a 4th grader, who heard it from another 4th grader, who heard it from…" Then I zoned out.

Let me address a few of the questions from your co-workers that you presented.

Tell Carol that my fellow teachers and I have banned the kids from going out to that sewer grate anymore, so the clown rumors have mostly subsided.

Let Tiffany know that Ella seems to be over her terror and doesn't appear to be afraid to go outside anymore.

Please pass on to Winter that the Rampaging Clown never actually hurled chicken fingers at the kids in any of the stories I heard.

After school today, one of our math tutors, a retired teacher named Mrs. Eastgate, came into my room to tell me a funny story. She's been working with a few of my kids every day, and hopefully it's making a difference. She had read a word problem with the group that said, "Mary went to the store and bought 2 pairs of shoes. Each pair of shoes cost $25. How much money did Mary spend at the store?"

Mrs. Eastgate told me that after hearing the problem, Franco had leaned over to her and whispered, "Mary should have gone to the Family Dollar store."

That's a very thoughtful observation from Franco, and it might be a reflection of the type of critical thinking I've been trying to get during science class where we've been talking about changes to the environment. Changes on a global scale that is, not localized changes like Larry passing gas in your cubicle.

Today, I gave the kids a quiz called "Helpful or Harmful?" I gave them a list of events that could happen, and they had to decide whether it was helpful or harmful to that environment. They also had to write down some way that that event would change the environment.

For instance, the first event was, "Trees are cut down to build new houses." For the most part, the kids agreed that this would be harmful to the environment. I was very impressed with Tomas, who said that one effect this would have on the environment would be to reduce the amount of oxygen available. Some of the other responses were not quite as impressive, but still memorable. Here are a few.

Event: Filling up a pond to make a parking lot.
Responses:
"Harmful, because the frogs would have no place to swim the fish would die and turn into fossils."
"Harmful, because the fish live there and they wanted their home."
"Helpful – putting cement is helpful because it's making the water clean."
I think someone has cement confused with fluoride.

Event: Collecting old newspapers in the neighborhood for recycling.
Responses:
"Helpful because it will make less trash on the floor."
"Helpful – so people can't read the newspapers anymore."
So by not reading math problems, the kids are actually trying to be helpful?

Event: A flood brings fertile soil to a river bank.
Responses:
"Harmful – the river bank will look gross."
"Harmful – a flood is bad, it mostly comes from the toilet and it can be very nasty n-a-s-t-e and it can ruin the soil on the land."
"Harmful – no one would be able to pay money at the river bank."
That last one was my favorite response on the entire quiz.

Event: Building a bird house and feeder in your backyard.
Best response:
"Harmful – garden will be destroyed."
Well sure, if you let the folks from Extreme Home Makeover: Bird Feeder Edition take the job!

I found it both fun and insightful to read the kids' thoughts on this quiz. And now here's one for you. Was Victor being Helpful or Harmful?

On our way out to the playground today after lunch, Victor was walking alongside me. He glanced over and asked, "Mr. Woodson, what happened to your balls?"

Honestly, I wasn't quite prepared for that one, and I had no idea how to respond. Somehow resisting the urge to look down at or grab my crotch, I asked, "Excuse me?"

He nonchalantly continued, "How come we don't take your basketballs outside anymore?"

Relief washed over me, so much so that I almost said, "Oh, because I didn't feel like you guys were handling my balls with the proper respect."

Instead, I figured I would leave the (intentional) double entendres for classic Saturday Night Live skits.

TGIF!

Talk to you later,

Balzac Johnson

Hey dude,

I learned over the weekend that Jill has never seen any of the Star Wars movies! I was trying to impress her by telling her about my YouTube video, Darth Vader Explains the Pythagorean Theorem, but I hit a wall. I guess there's no point in telling her about my sequel ideas – Han Solo Demonstrates a Fourier Transform, Boba Fett Proves the Quadratic Equation, or Yoda Discusses Unified String Theory.

She hasn't seen these movies YET, anyway. My plan to sit her down with the original trilogy is absolutely Helpful, whereas it sounds like Latya's excessive use of his new goatee wax is undoubtedly Harmful.

Also Harmful was the decision by Patrick, my new Behavioral Unit charge, to feel up the new teacher's assistant today. The poor girl has only been here a week, and already she's been groped by a nine-year-old. Welcome to the jungle.

As a result, Patrick has been de-mainstreamed and will no longer be joining Felicia in my class for science.

Patrick's actions are very controversial, and I'm about to make a very controversial statement myself. I'm starting to believe that Matthew, Mark, Luke, and John were not very good at math. Yeah, I'm talking about THAT Matthew, Mark, Luke, and John.

I've been working on multiplication and division word problems with my students, and I've noticed a striking similarity between some of their answer choices and a famous story from the New Testament.

Just imagine if this was a word problem, posed to the young gospel writers:

"Jesus has 5 loaves of bread. He wants to split the bread equally among 1,000 people who are hungry. How many loaves of bread will each person receive?"

Now, if MML&J tackled this problem the way many of MY students would, they would multiply 5 times 1,000 and get 5,000.

Each person will receive 5,000 loaves of bread.

No wonder everyone ate to their fill and there was a multitude still left over!

In the case of the Gospel story, this is referred to as a miracle, and I happen to believe in its veracity. Not so much with my kids.

On the test I gave last Friday, one question was, "Mrs. Martin has 30 pieces of candy. She wants to give the same amount of candy to 10 students. How many pieces of candy will each student get?"

Every time I saw an answer of 300 (or 40, from my kids who still think that adding is the only way to solve any math problem), I kept wanting to exclaim, "Hallelujah! It's a MIRACLE!!"

It's one thing to try to teach problem solving skills and operational procedures. Trying to teach logical thinking and common sense, though, is another (nearly impossible) thing entirely. Back to the Helpful or Harmful conceit, it would be so very Helpful if the FDA would hurry up and develop a drug called Logitrex, because so many of the kids at my school seem to be allergic to thinking!

This morning, I was trying to explain to the kids why the answer to one word problem did not make sense. The question was something along the lines of, "Herbert is 19 years old. His sister is 17 years old. How much older is Herbert than his sister?"

Many of my kids had added the two numbers and gotten 36 as their answer. Franco had added the two numbers together and gotten 26. Of course, if Herbert was only 19 years old, he could not possibly be 36 years OLDER than anyone else. As a living example, I said to the kids, "I am 36 years old. The only person I am 36 years OLDER than is..."

At this point, Priya raised her hand and blurted out, "ME??"

I continued, "is someone who was just born today. You might ACT like you were just born today, but we all know that's not really true."

Totally missing the point, Priya replied, "No, I was born April 1st."

All I could say was, "That sounds about right."

The other kids weren't interested in "Priya's a Fool" Day, though. As usual, the reveal of a teacher's age brought on more discussion than the latest Lady Gaga costume. (Never mind the fact that this is not the first time they have heard my age.)

"You're 36?!??"

"I thought you were 24!"

"I thought you were 100!"

And the one that really struck my fancy – "You look taller than 36."

Yes, children, I'm as tall as a 50-year-old. Way to restore my faith in your logical reasoning abilities.

Seriously, we need that Logitrex, STAT!! Because otherwise, it's going to take a miracle of Biblical proportions to help some of these kids pass the TAKS.

By the way, my balls are safe and secure, thanks for asking. Nancy asked about them as well, prompting me to send her a reply asking why she never writes to me about a NORMAL story.

See ya,

Tall McCartney

Date: Friday, February 5, 2010
To: Fred Bommerson
From: Jack Woodson
Subject: How I (FINALLY!) met your mother

Hey Fred,

I think you're right. If I brought Philby in to the classroom and asked the kids how old he was, they probably WOULD guess 12 or 14, if they were going by height.

And FYI, I was just using the loaves and fishes story as an example. I never said I was going to create a mathematically-themed version of the Bible, so don't get excited. But no, if I did, I would NEVER call it the King Bommerson Revised Version.

Great news today! We finally managed to get Ta'varon and Demontrae's mom in for a conference! We've been trying to meet with her ever since the boys enrolled, with no luck. Phone messages went unanswered, and even though Mrs. Bird actually DID reach her twice, both times we were stood up with no explanation.

The most recent no-show was last Thursday, when she was supposed to meet us after school. Given her history, when she didn't appear, we were about as shocked as we were when we discovered the air in our classrooms was still breathable.

Then yesterday, I acquired The Phone.

I was sitting at the overhead machine going over a word problem when the electronic chirping began. Everybody in the room froze, in that special way that kids freeze when they anticipate someone getting busted.

It was clearly coming from Ta'varon's general area, and he stared wide-eyed at me with an expression that was one part, "I have no earthly idea why my pants are buzzing," and four parts, "Please don't break out the cattle prod!" I held out my hand expectantly to him, and he grudgingly gave the phone to me. I flipped it open and answered it, but the caller had already hung up. That didn't stop me from carrying on a one-sided conversation, though, as Ta'varon stood nervously in front of me.

"Hello? No, I'm sorry, this is Mr. Woodson, Ta'varon's math teacher. Ta'varon is in class right now and can't take any calls. Please don't call him between 7:30 and 3:30. Thank you. Goodbye."

Fortunately, Ta'varon didn't ask who had called, because I probably would have answered something ridiculous, like Sponge-Bob Squarepants or Cobra Commander.

I asked Ta'varon why he had a cell phone at school. He insisted that it wasn't his, that someone had dropped it outside, and he had just picked it up. I wasn't convinced. So a little while later, while the kids were busy, I pulled up the phone's contact list and looked through the numbers. Under one listed as "Granny," there was a number with a 620 area code. Kansas. Ta'varon and Demontrae are FROM Kansas. Coincidence? I think not.

I walked across the hall and pulled Demontrae out of Mrs. Bird's class. I showed him the phone, told him I had found it, and asked if he knew whose it was.

With a sneer, he informed me that it belonged to his older brother who was in middle school.

BUSTED!!

Needless to say, Ta'varon immediately lost recess privileges for a couple of days. But more importantly, I now had a phone with a listing for "Ma."

After school, I dialed the number and was greeted with a somewhat angry, "What you callin' me now for?"

I identified myself and told her that we missed seeing her on Thursday. In a much more subdued voice, she offered an excuse. "Yeah, I been feeling a bit sick. Cough, cough."

Yes, my friend, she actually fake coughed in an attempt to validate her claim.

Pretending I didn't hear that part, I told her we'd still like her to come up to the school to talk with us, and now also to pick up the cell phone. She said she'd come the next day.

I asked her to show up by 3:30. "Don't come in too late, because sometimes I get sleepy after school. Yawn."

Imagine my shock when I actually got called out of class this morning around 8:30 to meet with her and Ms. Zapata, the assistant principal, in the conference room. Demontrae and Ta'varon were also there.

In a nutshell, the conference lasted about twenty minutes and included the bold, if somewhat suspect, statement from the mother that Demontrae would be going back to Kansas to live with his father in about two weeks. I'll believe that when I see it. Cough, cough.

Ta'varon can certainly be troublesome at times, but there's just something about the kid that makes me like him. At the end of anything that involves writing, where most kids write, "The End," Ta'varon writes, "Have a great day." He laughs at my jokes. He participates in class. He gets along well with his classmates. He's ok. He's just lazy, like so many of the others.

Demontrae, on the other hand, is mean and sullen. He never has a kind word and acts like a caged animal. If he really is moving out of state, I'd love to help him pack.

I did make it perfectly clear during the conference that cell phones are not allowed in class. In fact, the only instance a child would ever need to use a cell phone in my class would be to call for help if I was on the floor being eaten by a cougar.

And the class I have this year has already proven that they wouldn't call 911 in such a case. They'd move closer to the cougar! Talk to you later,

Arthur Phonezerelli

Date: Tuesday, February 9, 2010
To: Fred Bommerson
From: Jack Woodson
Subject: Heinz-way robbery

Hey Fred,

You really didn't have to include the phrase, "Clickety clack" after EVERY sentence. I pretty much understood that you were composing an email after the first few times. Way to commit and follow through to the end, though. This is definitely resume gold.

I most definitely support your resolution to end every technical paper with "Have a great day" from now on. I'll be sure to let Ta'varon know that he was such an inspiration. I know that Paul, Reggie, and Bert will be relieved that you've stopped writing "The End" at the close of every memo.

Today was filled with more turns and surprise twists than M. Night Shyamalan's small intestine.

While entering the classroom this morning, Ava asked me, "Is it true you love –" and she said something that I couldn't quite understand. It sounded like "cupchup," and I wondered for a moment if I was speaking with an Ewok. Asking her to repeat the question didn't clear it up for me. It was still, "Do you love cupchup?"

I finally broke down and asked her, "What is cupchup?"

Several other kids chimed in with, "Ketchup!!"

While understanding dawned on my face, Ava looked a little peeved and said, "That's what I said! Cupchup!"

Apparently, Mrs. Bird used me as an example in a graphic organizer yesterday. She was teaching the kids to make a chart with the Main Idea in a big box and three supporting details in smaller boxes. In her example, "Mr. Woodson" was the main idea, and the three details were "Tall," "Math teacher," and "loves ketchup on macaroni & cheese."

The timing of her sample poster could not have been more perfect – or ironic, depending on how you look at it. While the kids were now familiar with my affinity for the red nectar, I discovered today that not everyone in the cafeteria was.

I had an incident at lunchtime with a lady that I had never seen before and whom I hope never to see again. She was some kind of food services big wig from the district, and I didn't catch her name, so I'll just call her "The Ketchup Nazi."

I didn't bring my lunch today, so I bought it from the cafeteria. They were serving hamburgers and mac & cheese. I'm a growing boy, so I got both. Then I grabbed a handful of ketchup packets and put them on my tray. When I got to the cash register, I encountered the Ketchup Nazi.

She looked disapprovingly at my tray and said, "Sir, you are allowed one ketchup packet per item, and additional packets will cost 25 cents each."

I replied the way I think anyone would have – "Are you kidding me??!?!" (Notice I very politely did not include the word "effing.")

She did not respond favorably to that, so I grudgingly went back to the counter and put all but two of the packets back. But when I returned to the cash register, the Ketchup Nazi still gave me grief! She said that the mac & cheese did not count as an "item," and therefore I could only have one packet free of charge.

I suddenly had an overwhelming desire to hurl chicken fingers and epithets at this woman.

I choked all of that down, though, paid for my meal, and walked away with my complimentary quarter-ounce condiment door prize. But then, something wonderful happened. As I passed by my classes, Katie, sitting on the end of the table, offered me her ketchup. Seeing this, Ava offered me hers as well. As did Temperance, and Jacob, and Isabel, and even Victor!

Wow. I mean, wow. Some of these kids frustrate the hell out of me, but talk about selflessness. They really know the way to touch my heart.

Later today, I got to have more fun with some of them. Today is Tuesday, which means enrichment day, and we would normally play basketball. However, since it was rainy today (no outdoor activities) and the gym was occupied, we joined Mrs. Bird's Games Club in her room. I spent the entire hour playing two favorites of the kids – Uno and Connect Four.

Playing Uno with the kids was hilarious. They spent most of their time peering over the tops of their cards, looking like the poodles in the famous poker painting, and they never tracked whose turn it was. When it was someone's turn, I would look at him, and he'd get squinty eyed like I was about to call his bluff. I had to verbally remind almost everyone when they needed to play a card.

I could inevitably count on Eddie to try to play a red 3 on top of a blue 7. In the first game, I had to be the one to burst his bubble when he had one card left, there was a green 4 on top of the discard pile, and he giddily laid down his last card with a look of triumph on his face and shouted, "Khan-tay!"

"Um, Eddie, you can't play that yellow skip card now."

It's a really good thing we weren't playing poker, or anything for money for that matter, because these kids can't hide their cards OR their emotions. They're about as subtle as a radioactive eighty-foot-tall lizard wrecking downtown Tokyo. As the cards were dealt out one by one to begin a new game, the kids greeted each card with a cry of, "YESSS!!" or, "I GOT MY FAVORITE CARD!!" Whenever I played a wild card and changed the color, I was serenaded with either, "THANK YOU, MISTER WOODSON!" or, "NOOOOOOOO!!! NOT RED!!"

Really and truly, though, despite the fact that it makes for a longer day, I do enjoy seeing these kids out of the context of my classroom, where I tend to get frustrated with them easily. I like being able to take a step back and play games with them, instead of chastising them for adding two amounts of money to find change or calling a cube a triangle.

Plus, I can totally kick their butts at Connect Four, and even better, they're never going to charge me 25 cents for a packet of ketchup.

Later,

Tom Ayto

Date:	Friday, February 12, 2010
To:	Fred Bommerson
From:	Jack Woodson
Subject:	Be Mimes

Hey dude,

Has anyone ever told you that you have a very devious mind? I'm not really sure I agree with you that it would have been worth a dollar to buy four packets and "accidentally" squirt them on the Ketchup Nazi. The kids are still getting over an imagined monster from one Stephen King movie, after all. Do we really want to recreate the Prom scene from Carrie in the cafeteria?

Hey, you know what this Sunday is, right? To quote Charles Dickens, "It was the best of times, it was the worst of times, it was Valentimes."

I just can't seem to get across to my kids that this is not how you pronounce Valentines! They all say it wrong. Just like ketchup becomes "cupchup" and pizza is "pixa." Oh well, when our own principal pronounces "segue" as "seg-yoo," maybe I shouldn't worry too much about enforcing correct pronunciation with the kids.

Speaking of cupchup, how can you still not understand why ketchup is so important to me? It's like my fellow Virginian, Patrick Henry, once said, "Give me ketchup, or give me death!"

Sure, everybody knows he really said, "liberty," but what most folks don't realize is that Liberty™ was the Colonial version of Heinz.

Since Valentine's Day is on Sunday, we had our school party today. I now have enough candy to last until the end of the world (Thanks a lot, Ancient Mayans!).

Wednesday, I sent home a flier with the kids that included a class list, so that they would be able to bring a card and/or goodies for everyone, and no one would feel left out. There's nothing worse than to be sitting at a desk with one lowly Snickers bar, while the kid next to you can't see over the pile of candy and mushy cards.

Before the kids left my room, though, I had them write in huge letters, "PARTY ON FRIDAY." I told them repeatedly NOT to bring snacks until Friday.

Lo and behold, at 7:20 yesterday morning, the first kid through the door was Victor, carrying a big box of homemade cupcakes. Victor is not exactly the freshest Rice Krispie Treat in the pan. When I reminded him that the party was on Friday, and that he himself had written that note on his flier, he said, "I know! But my mom said I had to bring them today!"

The cupcakes were in a shallow cardboard box, covered with a sheet of tinfoil. I was very tempted to start a class science project this morning, to examine the effects of oxidation on yeast, as in cupcakes left out on a shelf. Instead, I went to the cafeteria and got some plastic wrap, and the snacks were able to survive until today.

Victor wasn't alone. He was the only one who brought edible foodstuffs, but several other boys brought cards. Their listening skills just never cease to amaze me.

We had shortened classes today and started our party around 1:30. I wanted to pass out little candy hearts with messages like, "Kick some math!" and, "Signs does matter!" but I just couldn't find any at the store. Instead, I got a couple boxes of Star Wars and Spiderman cards to give to the kids while they passed out their cards and goodies.

A few highlights from the party:

Lex and Tyler did not bring ANYTHING for anybody else, yet they sat at their desks shouting, "I didn't get one of those yet!!" at the kids who were passing out goodies.

Nestor, who couldn't read the names that his mom had printed on the Valentines, kept coming up to me and asking, "Mr. Woodson, who is this one for? Who is THIS one for?"

Lakeisha and my new kid, Charles, brought ginourmous bags of Hot Cheetos and shared them by dumping a pile on each desk.

Betsy showed up with what looked like pink eye, but the nurse cleared her in the morning. At the party, Betsy handed out cupcakes and frosted cookies, putting her hands all over them as she went. Hopefully my class on Monday will not look like a bad Polaroid picture.

I overheard Charles turn down one of Betsy's cupcakes, telling her, "I can only eat things that are sugar-free."

First of all, it's odd to hear the words "sugar-free" coming from ANY child at my school, but it's odder still to hear it coming from THIS kid, whom I've lovingly dubbed "The Round Mound of Sound."

Katie gave me a really cute little teddy bear that just might find itself regifted to a certain teacher very shortly.

Speaking of said teacher, I asked Jill last week if she could go to dinner on Sunday night, but she said her mother would be in town. Undaunted, I decided to do something romantic anyway, and I ordered flowers to be delivered to her today at her school. I picked out a lovely arrangement of multi-colored tulips and included a note that said, "I'm really enjoying getting to know you. Love, Jack."

Brownie points for me, right?

Maybe so, if they had actually been delivered. I spent the whole day hoping to get a nice little text from Jill saying she loved the flowers. Instead, at 3:15, I got a message from the flower place saying that their shipment had run late, but that they would make it up to me by making a special Saturday delivery tomorrow – free of charge.

It's to a school, numbnuts!! Nobody will be there tomorrow!!! AAAAARRRRRGGGHHHHH!!!!!

So why am I emailing you when I should be following up on this travesty? Good question.

Talk to you later,

Captain Dateless

Date:	Monday, February 15, 2010
To:	Fred Bommerson
From:	Jack Woodson
Subject:	Sock hop or hoedown?

Hey Fred,

Thanks for sending me that link to the site that sells custom-made candy hearts! I just might have some printed up next year! I really wish that you had ordered some with your funny phrases. My favorite was "Pete Humps Unlimited."

Payroll Pete would have loved it!

I finally did get Jill's flowers tracked down and picked up, though I had to go to the FedEx hub to get them. So I'll be hand-delivering them at our V-day make-up dinner on Wednesday evening. Not quite the surprise I had planned, but still romantic nonetheless.

The romance will have to wait till then, though, because I've still got these kids to deal with in the meantime. One less than before, actually, as Ta'varon announced loudly this morning that his brother had moved back to Kansas. I'm a bit stunned that it really happened and Demontrae is truly gone, especially since Ta'varon is still here. However, stranger things have happened, and I still have plenty of challenges to keep me on my toes.

Case in point – Lex, one of my extremely hyperactive, misbehaved, needy little boys, asked me a very interesting question today. So of course I gave him a very interesting answer right back.

He asked, "Mister Woodson, why do some people grow up to be bank robbers?"

I could hardly help but give the answer I did.

"Well, Lex, those people just never learned to make good choices. It probably started with them making very bad choices in the third grade, like stealing pencils, lying to their teacher, and touching people in bad places. Then they did things like that all the way through the rest of their school years. Which is why it's so important to start making good choices NOW, when you're still in the third grade."

I have no doubt that deep down, underneath that boisterous, uninterested-looking exterior, Lex forgot he had even asked me a question midway through my answer.

This morning in science class, we watched a short online

video called "Sock Seeds." In it, two kids put socks over their shoes then went outside and walked around for awhile in an open field. When they took their socks off, they observed all of the seeds that their socks had picked up. The kids then "planted" one of the socks in a shoe box filled with potting soil, watered it, and declared that in a few short weeks, they would have a small garden sprouting from the sock seeds.

At the point in the video where the little girl started to bury the sock in the soil, Lance realized what was happening and enthusiastically told the child next to him, "That's where they get socks from!"

I have no doubt that he will go home tonight and bury a dollar bill in his back yard in the hopes that a wonderful money tree will grow.

Still, his confusion pales by comparison to this afternoon's hysteria from another third grader. Mrs. Fitzgerald and Mrs. Frisch could barely get through telling me the story after school today, they were laughing so hard.

They have a little girl named Un'Kommon, who had a bit of a fit in the library today.

Yeah, that's her name. I'm guessing she does not have any siblings named Subtle or Low-key.

Mrs. Frisch had taken her class to the library after lunch where Mrs. Drogz, the librarian, read a story to them. This story involves a grandmother raising her granddaughter out on a farm. At a moment of conflict in the story, the gentle folk are threatened by a rattlesnake. The grandmother tells the girl that she is going to get a hoe to fend off the snake.

The instant that line was spoken, Un'Kommon got wide-eyed and blurted out, "She sinned!!"

Mrs. Drogz, utterly befuddled, tried to explain, "No, sweetie, the grandmother was just trying to protect the little girl. That's why she needed to get the hoe."

But Un'Kommon insisted, "NUH-UH!!! SHE'S A SINNER!!!!"

Apparently, the poor girl was not aware of an alternate meaning (and spelling) of the critical word that she had heard. Garden implement, dear child, NOT lady of ill repute.

I'm thinking someone needs to very carefully screen all stories for potentially inflammatory terms from now on. After all, a wise man once said that people's lives are strongly influenced by

what they do in third grade. I'd hate for any of our kids to grow up to be a hoe, a stud finder, or a tool of any sort for that matter.
Talk to you later,

The Scarlet Pimp-ernel.

Date:	Thursday, February 18, 2010
To:	Fred Bommerson
From:	Jack Woodson
Subject:	Badgies?? We don't need no steenkin' badgies!!

Hey buddy,

When you start off your email with the sentence, "I myself have found a good use for a hoe on several occasions," I have to wonder if I should be sharing Un'Kommon's reaction. Larry bringing up TJ Hooker is pretty darn funny. I can only hope Un'Kommon doesn't watch many old, crappy shows from the '80s.

I've noticed that one of my little girls, Priya, seems to have a particular fondness for corners. She obviously loves spending time in the corner of MY room, because she's constantly doing things that land her there. Frequently when I pick the class up after lunch, Priya has her nose in the cafeteria corner. When I get the class from PE, she's closely examining one corner of the gym.

Today when I saw Priya in the art room corner, I told Mr. Vann that I might need to help her write a brand new book that would showcase her unique interests. I suggested a Fodor's-style travel guide, maybe "200 Classroom Corners in 175 Days."

I'm sure that Priya would be able to provide some useful insights into which corners smell the best, which corners are most aesthetically pleasing, and which corners are most likely to provide habitats for creepy-crawlies.

Speaking of writing, the very last activity that we did today during after-school tutoring was a writing exercise, and I know that my brother Zack would appreciate this one. I passed out some leftover Spiderman valentine cards to the kids and told them to write a story based on the card's picture. Misspellings aside, it was entertaining to read some of the kids' stories and find that Spidey can fly, he can roundhouse kick people in the face a la Chuck Norris, and he likes to go around yelling, "I AM SPIDERMAN!" Just in case people don't recognize him from the costume.

Big Jack had written a story about Spidey fighting a handful of "badgies." Badgies (pronounced "Bad Guys" by the author; pronounced "Badgies" by all others) were a staple of my brother's elementary school writing period. All stories followed a specific formula. Goodgies fight badgies. Badgies go to jail. End of story.

Sometimes the setting varied (castle, big castle, red castle), but the plot always remained the same.

And really, Hollywood has followed suit. Die Hard on a plane. Die Hard on a mountain. Die Hard on Sharon Stone.

This was the first time I had seen Big Jack or any of my students writing about badgies. I won't make any comments like, "Please stop writing the same story!" (actual note on my brother's 7th or 8th paper) unless he recycles the plot a few times.

Thinking of notes in red on writing assignments makes me think back to my junior year chemistry class in high school. We had a standing weekly assignment to find and cut out a science-related article and to write a one-page summary.

It was well-documented that our teacher only glanced at the first sentence of the paper and gave grades based on that. So every week, my friends and I had a contest to see who could submit the wildest, most redonkulous papers.

A typical paper might read as follows:

"NASA has developed a new, innovative way to protect astronauts from over-exposure to UV radiation during manned space flights. This was never performed on monkeys when NASA shot Bozo the chimp up to the moon, but people are another case. My throat feels scratchy when I eat potato chips, and Vodka is a funny sounding word. Is my grandmother supposed to snicker when she breaks wind? Elizabeth Taylor kind of scares me, but my dad likes her. Dog food and horse doodles, I always say."

And so on, and so on, for a full page. Every time, our papers would come back with a check plus.

It came as quite a shock when our chem teacher was fired over Christmas break that year (possibly related to his lax grading standards, though the rumor was always that he was caught in flagrante delicto with a senior cheerleader), and a new teacher arrived.

This new teacher kept the old assignment, and whereas MOST of us began to write an actual page-long review of our article, one of my best friends pushed his luck the first week and continued with a nonsensical review.

I'll never forget how much red ink came back on his paper. Some of his sentences, like, "But there's still one thing that puzzles me – there is no mention of the crown jewels!" were repeatedly circled and surrounded by question marks.

Man, I wonder if any of my teachers back then sat down every couple of nights and wrote a letter to a friend, telling them all about me and her other weirdo students.

Nah, my old teachers probably just drank themselves silly.

As for Big Jack and his badgies, I think I'll write him a note encouraging him to serialize the adventures of his heroic protagonist. Maybe he'll become a famous screenwriter who creates the next big epic tale (and twenty successful sequels), and someday I'll get a call to play "Badgie Number 15."

Later,

Scott Baio-Wolf

Date: Tuesday, February 23, 2010
To: Fred Bommerson
From: Jack Woodson
Subject: A little vocabulary lesson

Hey dude,

Sorry you've been sick for the past few days. I would think some of those badgies you work with would make anyone nauseous. Just be happy that you can call in sick without having to make plans or arrange for a replacement, like I do.

I wasn't sick, but since my birthday fell on a Sunday this year, I decided to take yesterday off. It just so happens that yesterday was marked on the classroom calendar as President's Day. So today, when the association was made between my birthday and the holiday, Jessie started up a rousing cheer of, "Vote for Mr. Woodson!"

Most of the other kids just stared at him as if his pants were on backwards.

This afternoon, I stayed late – too late – at school. I had taken up my students' science journals to grade something they had written, and I didn't want to lug all the journals home and back. What made my stay even later was that two of my former students came in asking if they could do anything to help me around the room.

I gave them a stack of homeworks that I hadn't graded yet and an answer key. However, they seemed a lot more interested in talking, so there wasn't a whole lot of grading going on.

The boys told me that a little girl in Mr. Redd's class had been suspended for bringing alcohol to school. Naturally, I asked, "What kind of alcohol did she bring?"

One of the boys replied, "The white kind!"

And thus began the vocabulary lesson for the boys, as I rattled off a litany of possibilities, trying to hit on the white alcohol in question.

"Vodka? Rum? Everclear? Zima? Peach Schnapps? Triple Sec?"

Afterwards, I was glad they had not said someone brought drugs to school. I could see myself grilling the kids:

"Was it marijuana? Coke? Cheese? Heroine? Yellow jackets? Speedballs? Goofballs? Ludes? Shrooms? X? Spanish Fly? Spinach?"

I asked Mr. Redd about it later, and he told me that the alcohol in question was an airline travel-size bottle of Bacardi Rum. What Larry would call "Breakfast."

Do you remember that time we flew out to the convention in Anaheim, and Larry drank so much on the flight that he was actually cut off? He had finished off two bottles of rum and was trying to order a third when the flight attendant told him no, adding, "Sir, it's 10:30 in the morning."

He had certainly been sober enough the night before, when he called the airline to reserve a Kosher meal in my name.

Back to today, I may not have immediately guessed the contraband liquid in the afternoon, but earlier in the day, I was finally acknowledged as being smart. I mean REALLY smart. We're talking Earth-shattering GENIUS here!

Well, at least according to my kids.

This morning, I picked my class up from art where Mr. Vann was waiting at the door. I reminded the kids that they should thank Mr. Vann for burning them all copies of the multiplication CD.

The kids thanked him and then started singing the 3's song, with me singing right along. There's a fun little ditty that lists all of the multiples – 3, 6, 9, 12, 15, 18, 21, 24, 27, 30.

By then, I was walking the kids down the hallway, and I added, "And don't forget 33 and 36!"

Even though the songs stop at ten times the number, I test the kids up to twelve times the number since that's what they'll need to know for fourth grade.

As we walked, Tyler asked, "Mister Woodson, do you know 3 times one million?"

I said, "Yes, it's 3 million."

About five kids in line gave an awed, "WHOAAAAA" – the same sound uttered by a crowded stadium when Blake Griffin jumps over a car and delivers a tomahawk dunk.

Ava then asked, "Do you know SIX times one million??"

Warming to my audience, I replied with a flourish, "But of course – 6 million!"

By now there were murmurings in the line that I might be the second coming.

Felipe then pulled out his big guns. He asked, "Mister Woodson, do you know what is four... plus... three?"

I was a bit surprised by the simplicity of his question, but I replied, "Um, yeah, seven."

"Oh yeah!!" Felipe exclaimed, with a beatific smile on his face, as if I had just told him the meaning of life, and it involved never having to read again and an endless supply of Hot Cheetos.

If I had had a magician's smoke pellet, I could have thrown it down to the ground and disappeared to complete the grand act.

I suppose the lesson here is that I should focus on impressing the kids with my number sense, and not my knowledge of potent potables.

See ya,

Cal Q Later

Date: Friday, February 26, 2010
To: Fred Bommerson
From: Jack Woodson
Subject: No chain, no gain

Freddy,

Clearly you're just jealous that you don't have anyone in your life that is easily impressed by the ability to add single-digit numbers. Though you might try your luck showing off your division skills with Nancy up front. I hear she's got a thing for math nerds.

If you weren't just being sarcastic, I can certainly sing you the 3's song next time I see you. I'll warn you, however. Once you get it stuck in your head, that song will not go away. It's more pervasive than the Smurfs theme song!

For the past couple of weeks in science, our smurfing topic of discussion has been producers, consumers, and food chains. When I first asked the class what a food chain was, Jacob said, "It's where families go to eat on Valentine's Day."

Close, but no cigar. Not to be confused with FAST food chains, the regular run-of-the-mill type of food chains are those fun little paths that lead from producer to consumer. All chains start with a plant, followed by an animal that eats that plant, then an animal that eats THAT animal. A typical example might be as follows:

corn - chicken - person

It always takes me a while to convince my class that, in the science world, people are animals. Every year, there's at least one smarty pants who argues, "Nuh-uh! People are MAMMALS!!"

I usually combat this by stooping to their level.

Me: "Is Victor a human being?"
Kids: "YES!!"
Me: "Nuh-uh! Victor is a BOY!!"

I'm all about developing those critical thinking skills.

The producer/consumer concept just throws more gas on the fire. The fact that animals – and thus humans – cannot make their own food is another stumbling block for the kids. I always get a chorus of arguments.

"I can TOO make my own food! I can make a turkey sandwich, and sometimes my mommy lets me make spaghettios!"

I think I'll start showing Food Network videos in class, to highlight the difference between PRODUCING your food and PREPARING your food. Plants, and only plants, have the ability to create their own food through photosynthesis. My kids can slap a meal together, through a process I like to call dodosynthesis.

Anyway, last night, I gave an extra credit homework assignment which was to make and illustrate a food chain. I got some very interesting submissions. Here are a few proposed chains that we will not be seeing in nature anytime soon:

Corn - Lion - Shark
Unless it's a land shark, of course. Candygram!

Bananas - Monkey - Ape
That would be cannibalism, kids, and that's just wrong.

Apples - Horse - Me
At first, I thought she was saying she was hungry enough to eat a horse, but maybe she was making a reference to Jell-O?

Strawberry - Ferret - Fox - Brontosaurus
Silly kid! Now this is truly ridiculous. Brontosaurus is a PLANT eater!

Then there were several who just didn't get the concept at all.

Dog - Food - Pedigree - Flea spray
Um, FOOD chain, my dear girl, not product line.

Fan - Air - Energy
Wow, a metaphysical food chain!

Dog food - Dog - Car
I asked about this, and the writer told me it was because cars hit dogs sometimes.

And my first annual winner of the "No Clue Chain" Award...

Banana - Corn - Soup - Tomato - Apple - Popcorn chicken

This was accompanied by a picture with the caption, "This is Eddie eating corn and tomato and banana."
Check plus for making a chain of food; check minus for comprehending the actual concept.

Quite obviously, this lesson falls under the heading – RE-TEACH!
Still, it did give me my favorite food chain of all time:

Strawberry - Squirrel - Snake - Chinese person
Nice integration of Science and Social Studies from Smoker Anna, a born overachiever.

After lunch (during which time the kids fulfilled their role as top of the food chain), I received a formal observation. Once or twice a year, Mrs. Forest or Ms. Zapata comes and sits in on the class for 30-45 minutes. This is part of our yearly evaluation, but it always makes me nervous. Not that I have anything to hide – I'm always very careful to meticulously hide the weapons of math destruction – but I hate speaking in front of adults. Throw me in front of a thousand kids and I'm fine, but add a grown-up or two to the mix, and I suffer a massive anxiety attack. You may remember the deep shade of fire engine I always turned when asked to give my status update at production meetings.
The observation went pretty well I thought. I did my best to keep Shelly from writing notes, Victor from visiting Planet Zorlon, and Joaqim from being overly Joaqimly. Two things did stand out, though.
First, Mia raised her hand to show me her answer to the problem of the day. I glanced at it, saw that it was correct, gave her a thumbs up, and said, "Very nice!"
She immediately replied with her patented and unique form of thank you – "YOU A GOOD TEACHER!!"
Maybe it was just my imagination that she said it twice as loud as normal, but I don't think so.
A little while later, Tyler made everyone aware that he had conquered the problem he was working on. He did this by slamming his hand down on his desk and shouting, "KHAN-TAY!"
I can only hope Mrs. Forest will appreciate my students' passion and excitement for learning. And that she won't ever ask

me to explain their thinking process. Linear food chains, I can handle. These kids' chains of thought – no clue.
Talk to you later,

Herb E Vorr

Hey dude,

I'm very saddened that you would make such a cruel food chain poster and put it in Latya's cubicle. I mean, really?

Excessive amounts of candy and potato chips - Latya

That's just wrong, dude.

It's wrong because all food chains are supposed to start with a plant. I thought I said that before.

Something else that might be wrong – I haven't talked to Jill in about a week and a half now. I've gotten a few short texts saying she's been busy, but that's about it. I'm trying not to read anything into this, but I'm starting to wonder if I should be worried.

I don't want to dwell on that, though, so I'll dive right into this week's brand new objective for third grade – capacity. The kids are of course unfamiliar with the topic, and it's a topic that I am pretty unfamiliar with myself. As a former engineer, I know a lot about measurement in terms of length and temperature, but I don't have much experience with pints and milliliters. There were a few questions I needed to answer before trying to teach the concept.

Why does the abbreviation for ounces have a "z" in it?

How many pints are there in a buttload?

Is it ever truly acceptable to use the word "dram" in civilized conversation?

Monday morning came with the anticipated confusion. For kids who have trouble remembering the difference between a square and a rectangle, capacity seemed doomed from the quart. I introduced the customary units first, but most of the units were words the kids had never even heard before. I may as well have said 2 snerks equals 1 plekt, and 8 crells in a doogy.

After the strange words had been introduced, though, I focused on real-world examples. I showed the kids a milk jug to represent a gallon and a Gatorade bottle to represent a quart. A peek into my home fridge led to the discovery that a bottle of Kraft ranch salad dressing holds exactly 1 pint, so I brought that in for show and tell as well. I found something that has a capacity of exactly 1 liter, but I opted to leave the bottle of Absolut at home.

Inspired by my own kitchen raid, I gave the kids an extra credit homework assignment last night. I asked them to go home and look through their refrigerators, freezers, and pantries. They may not have had a firm grasp on the concept of capacity, but I figured they could at least recognize the units on containers. They made lists of all of the containers they found, along with the capacity of each.

Reading through the lists today was one of the most entertaining things I've done in my classroom all year long. Maybe it's juvenile of me, but I laughed for almost ten minutes when I saw Tiny Anna's list, which included a "2-Liter bottle of Cock" (and Cock Zero!).

There were a few examples of missing decimal points – 612 gallons of barbecue sauce, 277 gallons of mustard, 118 liters of Mr. Clean. Either that, or someone owns stock in the wholesale store.

Soda and milk were on most lists, but items like Ms. Butterworth (1 pt, 8 oz), champagne (1.05 pt), and Hooter's hot sauce (5 fl oz) were unique. Perhaps with all of the varying liquids, it was inevitable that Maalox (355 mL) would make an appearance as well.

Most kids didn't limit themselves to food and drink alone. Lists included body oil (473 mL), Dawn dish soap (1.18 qt), and Tilex (1 pt).

After letting the kids have a few moments to share items from their lists with each other, I led them into the main part of today's lesson. I had something new that I wanted to try out.

A little while ago, I read a book called The Prisoner of Trebekistan. In it, former Jeopardy champion Bob Harris talks a lot about memory devices that he used while studying for the game show. His studying led him to the conclusion that things and events that make an outrageous or hilarious impression last the longest in memory. And it seems to have worked well for him.

That got me to thinking what sorts of humorous things I could do to try to leave a lasting mark in my students' memories. In other words, how many times can I make a complete fool of myself in the name of mathematic academics?

Let's start the ticker at one.

Today, I decided to be a Jedi. I took a quick poll and verified that all of my kids were familiar with Star Wars. Sadly, they were only acquainted with the Jar Jar Binks trilogy, but for the purposes of my lesson, I was able to work around that. Doing my best Obi-Wan Kenobi impersonation, I informed the kids that our new motto was going to be, "May the quarts be with you."

After we passed that mantra around a few times, I told them we could also say, "May the FOURTHS be with you."

Then we went over how this motto could help someone remember that there are four cups in a quart, and four quarts in a gallon, not to mention the fact that there are four letters in the words Jedi, Star, and Wars.

The kids in my morning class seemed to enjoy this immensely. Miles even pulled the hood of his jacket over his head, taking on the persona of a Jedi Knight, before doing a small bow and saying, "May the fourths be with you."

Most of the kids in my afternoon class, though, looked at me as though I was speaking Chinese or talking about subtraction.

Oh well, all it takes is that one connection. Besides, as they say, "Who's the more foolish – the fool, or the fool who follows him?"

Maybe tomorrow I'll introduce them to a Math Jedi's greatest weapon... the Pint-Saber.
Your friend,

Fearless Liter

Date:	Friday, March 5, 2010
To:	Fred Bommerson
From:	Jack Woodson
Subject:	Vision: Impossible

Hey dude,

I'm telling you, I don't even know how many pints are in a regular buttload. So how am I supposed to know how many pints are in a METRIC buttload?

After a full week, I'd say my kids have as firm a grasp on capacity as they are likely to get. At the very least, I feel confident that none of them will ever walk into a liquor store later in life and ask for five pounds of beer.

Somebody apparently wasn't happy with the capacity of a bottle of Elmer's glue. I learned this the hard way out at the bus line this afternoon. My bus started to pull away from the curb, and there was a tremendous BANG. I quickly realized two things: first, somebody had positioned a bottle of glue under the back tire of the bus, and second, my pants were covered in glue.

I was not a happy camper. Quite frankly, I'm STILL pretty ticked off about it, so rather than subject you to my anger, I'll switch gears and talk about something more ridiculous (though par for the course).

Yesterday, Shelly presented me with a very odd statement. I've come to expect odd statements from her, but this was odd even by her standards. We had just returned to my classroom after the restroom break that follows recess. Which means that it was around 12:45, and Shelly had already been in my room for an hour before lunch and recess.

It wasn't until that moment, however, that she chose to inform me, "Last night, I was watching TV, and it blinded me. I can't see my paper." Her paper, of course, being the math journal on her desk, a foot and a half from her face.

As you might imagine, I was a bit skeptical. I mean, when MY television blinds ME late at night, I don't get my vision back temporarily in the morning and then lose it again after lunch. Heck, even Han Solo didn't come out of his Carbonite suspension just fine only to go blind a day later.

Shelly persisted, however, and wouldn't do any of her work, so I finally took her across the hall to Mrs. Bird's room. I asked her if Shelly had done any of her reading and social studies work that morning, or if she had been too blind. Mrs. Bird is either used to our kids doing crazy things OR me asking crazy questions, so she wasn't fazed at all by our visit. She responded like a consummate professional that Shelly had appeared to have perfect vision and had done all of her work.

In the hallway, before we reentered my classroom, I tried a new tact. I told Shelly that Mrs. Fitzgerald had commented on how nice it was that Shelly had picked some flowers for her during recess. I added that it would be very difficult for someone to pick flowers and make a nice little bouquet if that someone was vision-impaired.

Shelly stared at me blankly (yes, this IS the same girl who calls me Miss Woodson) and finally said, "But... But some of the flowers were upside down!"

Is that one of the sure signs of blindness or something? "Flowers were upside down – driver's license denied!"

I didn't get much work out of Shelly for the rest of the day, but I had a talk with her parents last night, and thankfully, I didn't hear any more claims of blindness today.

From HER, that is...

Today, most of our kids went outside for recess, but I kept a small group of misbehaviors in my room. When my class came back inside, another little girl – Hillary – approached me and said, "Mister Woodson, I got pushed down outside on the playground and now I can't see. The nurse said I need to have someone in the classroom lead me around."

My students certainly won't be winning any prizes in originality any time soon.

Hillary was really hamming it up, walking around like a zombie with her hands out in front of her. I half expected her to start feeling my face, saying, "Mr. Woodson, is that you?"

Not surprisingly, Hillary had no note from the nurse giving me the aforementioned instructions. Nurse McCaffrey ALWAYS sends the kids back with detailed notes to teachers. So I found her claim lacking a bit in an area I like to call "FACT."

A few moments later, Mrs. Bird walked into my room, so I asked her about Hillary's condition. She confirmed my suspicion that the nurse had indeed sent back a note that said that Hillary was perfectly fine. I didn't see it, but I believe the note actually included the observation, "No blindness detected whatsoever."

Here's hoping we can go one more week without any claims of sensory loss. Then Spring Break will be here, and the kids can be

as blind, deaf, mute, and numb as they want to be while they're at home. I suspect they'll still smell, though.
Later,

Sy Tenpaired

Date: Tuesday, March 9, 2010
To: Fred Bommerson
From: Jack Woodson
Subject: The 5th Horseman of the Apocalypse

Hey buddy,

You are spot on, once again. The kids may appear to go blind and deaf all the time, but they never seem to go mute. I do think it would be funny if you pretended to go blind the next time you don't have an answer for Reggie at a status meeting. If he calls BS, counter with, "But some of the heating elements were upside down!"

Ironically enough, the annual vision tests are being performed at the school this week. I don't know how Shelly and Hillary could possibly have known about it last week, but the timing could not have been more interesting.

My students' eyes were tested today. Amidst heavy laughter, the kids each had to put on a bulky, nerdy pair of glasses and try to read the eye chart. After a while, Nurse McCaffrey asked me to either stop giggling or to leave the room.

At the end of the day, I witnessed the worst reaction ever to a suggestion for eyeglasses. Eight notes went home to parents suggesting that their child needs glasses (including one to Lex, who already wears them!). Tiny Anna got such a letter and burst into tears. Tiny Anna is a smart sweet angel of a child, and her reaction really surprised me. She kept sobbing, "I don't WANT glasses! My mom doesn't WANT me to have glasses!"

When I asked her why, she said, "Because they can get broken!"

Inwardly, I wondered if she had ever been allowed to own anything outside of Silly Putty, but outwardly, I tried to console her by telling her that glasses just have to be taken care of, and that if they get broken by accident, they can always be replaced. But she acted as if someone had told her she was going to have to watch a 48-hour long marathon of Freddy Got Fingered and then perform her own interpretive dance version afterwards.

On the other end of the spectrum from Tiny Anna, I got a new kid in my class yesterday. His name is Marshawn, and his reputation precedes him. Big time. He didn't show up in my room until 10, and I later found out that this was because those first two hours were spent down in the principal's office where he was read the riot act upon first entering the building. Apparently, his old school couldn't get him out the door fast enough, but they were thoughtful enough to forward several complaints about him to our principal before he arrived. From what I've heard, his ultimate transgression at his old school was breaking a toilet.

Over the course of my life, I've heard of or seen several different ways to break a toilet, including:

Dropping a shot put from a height of six feet into the porcelain bowl.
Standing on the rim and jumping up and down (lid up for boys, down for girls).
Stuffing the pipe so full of something (toilet paper, jump ropes, school uniforms) that the toilet just explodes.

Marshawn said something about using a screwdriver. My initial thought was NOT that he used it to unscrew all of the hardware, but rather that he did a "Psycho" number on the bowl and pipes. Slash and chip, baby.

I can already tell that Marshawn is going to test the limits of my positive to negative feedback ratio. Experts say that for every teacher's comment that could be construed as negative – "Stop throwing chicken nuggets at people!" – there should be something like ten positive comments – "Your accuracy is coming along nicely!" Thus, the positive: negative ratio.

I've set myself a more modest goal; instead of 10:1, I'm attempting to maintain a 3:1 ratio. Even so, I've already had to get pretty creative with kids like Joaqim and Suzie.

"I love the way you're converting oxygen to carbon dioxide!"
"Your snoring hardly disturbed anybody today!"
"You're doing a great job making the top half of the class possible!"

Today, Marshawn came in and wouldn't do any work for me. He kept putting his head down and looking to the world like he was taking a nap. I introduced him to my rule of "Sleep in your bed, not in my classroom."

He immediately responded, "I stayed up all night watching a movie!"

Hmmm...well, Marshawn, that would certainly explain the need for sleep, but here's an idea. Maybe, and this is just me thinking out loud here, you SHOULDN'T watch late-night movies when you have to go to school the next morning. Make sense?

Turns out he'll be able to watch all the Cinemax he wants tonight and tomorrow night. Mrs. Bird had him suspended for the rest of the week. It's pretty amazing for HER – normally a very calm, patient teacher who doesn't get rattled easily – to suspend a kid who's only been here for two days. No sewage disruption yet at our school (at least not due to him), but he's been throwing out insults like they were homeworks with no names on them. He dropped an F-bomb over in her room, called several kids' mothers an unsavory word that rhymes with "witch," and told Charles, "That is the Mother Effing biggest stomach I have ever seen!"

Marshawn is no Olive Oyl himself, so this really is a classic case of the pot calling the kettle fat. And I looked and beheld a crazyhorse, and an insane rider sat upon him. Why do the lunatics always show up right before Spring Break?

Hey, before I sign off, I have some bad news. I've been in a terrible mood since the weekend, and it's not just from having my pants ruined by glue or getting a new challenge in class. I had a date with Jill on Saturday, and instead of being the grand night of catching up that I had hoped for, it wound up being the not so grand night of BREAKING up.

Long story short, an ex-boyfriend has moved back to town and wants to rekindle the flame, she's torn but needs to take some time to sort out her feelings, she doesn't want to keep me hanging, yadda yadda yadda.

Maybe I should have seen this coming, but I pretty much feel blindsided. Big time bummer. I thought things were going so well. At least I only have three more days of school to make it through before getting an entire week off in which to wallow in self pity. And chocolate pudding.

For now, I guess I'll go drown my sorrows in about six liters of Mountain Dew. All the while thankful that I don't have to get glasses or use broken toilets.

Later,

Lou Zerr

Date:	Friday, March 12, 2010
To:	Fred Bommerson
From:	Jack Woodson
Subject:	The teacher will see you now

Hey Fred,

Thanks, man. I appreciate your support during this rough patch. I also appreciate you guys sending me all of the Photoshopped pictures of hot celebrities asking me out. I'm not sure Jennifer Garner would have misspelled so many words, but I liked the intent of the message all the same. Maybe a gorgeous brown-eyed brunette COULD help me "get over my resent brakeup."

This whole week has dragged, but yesterday was an especially super long day. The blank stares... The same questions over and over... The never-ending tattling... That's right, last night was Parent-Teacher conference night! There has been some debate over the past few days as to which is less torturous – conference night or a 22-hour road trip to Montana with a rabid ferret in the backseat.

Last night followed the usual pattern for Parent-Teacher conferences. The parents of the really bad kids don't show up, the parents who DO show up are mainly told that their kid needs to read more at home, and somebody down the hall is screaming the lyrics to "Twinkle, Twinkle Little Star" at the top of their lungs. Okay, that last one is not usual. Oh, and since many of our parents don't speak English, we had to keep buzzing the office to send a translator down.

A couple of times, when there was no translator available, we had to settle for one of our students' older brothers. This made me wonder if they were accurately converting what we said, or channeling Mouth from The Goonies.

Us:	"Michael needs to read at home every night."
Translated as:	"Michael has been asking some very disturbing questions about monkeys."
Us:	"Michael has not been participating in class."
Translated as:	"Michael has been smoking macaroni and cheese."
Us:	"Michael did well on his last math test."
Translated as:	"Michael says there that Uranus consists mostly of slushy gases."

Of the parents who did show up, Thilleenica's were certainly the most memorable. They seemed VERY happy to be there and had more giggle fits than I could count. Also, it wasn't difficult to see that they had bloodshot eyes, and there was a weird odor coming from them.

Yep, they showed up stoned. The really bad thing was that Thilleenica was with them. She wasn't stoned at least, but I can't imagine her home life is a very good one.

At one point, Thilleenica's dad glanced over at Bubba, the Scottish nutcracker, and said, "Hey! We used to have one of those!"

Thilleenica's eyes widened and darted over to me. I caught her eye, smiled, and decided to remain mum on the matter.

Amir's mom showed up and brought her one-year-old daughter. Less than five minutes into our conference, the little girl toddled over to me and climbed into my lap, where she stayed for the rest of our meeting. Mrs. Bird snapped a picture, and my first thought was that Jill would really like to see it. But then I remembered...

Antonio's father wanted to know why his son's grades were so much worse in reading than they were in math. I told him about the restaurant coupons I've been giving Antonio as an incentive, and he said, "Oh, yes, he told us this was his reward for doing his math."

He then looked squarely at Mrs. Bird and asked, "So why aren't YOU giving him restaurant coupons?"

If the conferences had been tonight instead of last night, I'm afraid of the repercussions I might have faced for something that a lot of the kids were saying this afternoon. On our way back inside from recess, we passed Miss Phelps, a first grade teacher who had a lot of my kids two years ago. The kids swarmed around her and clamored for her attention, shouting that they had passed their latest multiplication test. A couple had (finally!) passed the 4's test, and several had passed the 6's and 7's tests. The most vocal, however, seemed to be the group who were yelling, "I passed my 8's test!"

If that means nothing to you, it's because you're reading this silently. Try this – stand up at your desk right now and shout, "I passed my 8's test!" at Tiffany over the cubicle wall. See what happens. What looks commendable on paper is actually quite cringe-worthy out loud.

OK, man, I'm turning in for the night. By the time you read this, I'll already be dead. Wait, that's not right. By the time you read this, I'll already be three days into Spring Break! I'll come pester you guys for lunch a couple of times, if I feel like waking up before noon.

And if I'm not too busy giving Jennifer Garner private spelling lessons.

Later,

Ty Moff

Date: Tuesday, March 23, 2010
To: Fred Bommerson
From: Jack Woodson
Subject: Love letters from Dr. Jekyll

Hey buddy,

Spring Break is unfortunately over. You can officially cease your complaining now. The week off couldn't have come at a better time, and I took advantage of being a bum and not doing much. In addition to hanging out with you guys, a couple of the fourth grade teachers – Hank Redd and Spencer Utoobay – took me out one night and did their darndest to push me towards every attractive female in the bar. I learned quickly that the best way to get over one rejection is NOT to put yourself in line for several more.

But hey, I'm really feeling a lot better after having this time off. Especially after watching 172 straight hours of college basketball. NOTHING will ever dampen my enjoyment of March Madness!!

Thanks also for all of the support I've gotten from you and my other pals at HPU. I received a lot of very encouraging emails from lots of people. Don't ever tell him that I told you this, but I have to say I was most impressed with Larry. Dropping the horn-dog, goofball act for once, he sent me a surprisingly candid message about how he was able to get over the devastation of his divorce. My situation is nowhere near as extreme as that, but I was touched by his heartfelt words of advice.

So no more moping about Jill. Instead, I'll get back to rubbing in the fact that I just had a whole week off from work!! Don't you just love how that happens every year? Well, hey, you should be glad you don't have to come back from a nice vacation to anything crazier than Latya hung over.

I'll get to the classroom craziness later, but let's start with some madness! Like I said, March Madness is in full effect, and my brackets are looking pretty darn good. Duke's gonna win it all this year!!

In my class, the March Mathness tourney is just getting started. When I first asked the kids if any of them watched college basketball or had heard of March Madness, they looked at me as blankly as they do when I ask who knows what congruent means. There were a few nods of recognition and gasps of excitement, though, when I held up the brackets and announced the tournament.

I shouldn't be too surprised that the kids are unaware of March Madness, as sad as that might be. When I was still at Heat Pumps Unlimited, I once suggested a March Madness celebration to the Party Planning Committee. All of the ladies on the committee were very excited about it. I then had to explain to them that March Madness was a sporting event and not a once-a-year shopping extravaganza.

I had the kids draw numbers out of a basket to decide which slot their names would go in in the opening round of our contest. This morning, when I called Eddie up to the basket and he pulled a 6, there was a general, "OOOOOH!" from the rest of the class. Never mind the fact that his opponent had not yet been selected. The other numbers and slots generated the same reaction, and now the first round is set. The kids are excited and seem to be looking forward to the test on Friday. We'll see if that translates into better test scores or just more trash talking from kids like Tyler and Lex.

I myself didn't trash talk anyone at school today, but I did talk ABOUT trash with one parent. Priya's mom stopped by my classroom before lunch, upset about a note she had found in her daughter's possession. Mrs. Bird was with her, and she showed me the ragged little note that looked like it had been put through the washer.

Priya's mom was appalled that a boy in my class had written this note to Priya, and Priya had apparently told her mom that this boy was putting unwanted attention on her. Upon reading the note for myself, I wasn't so sure.

At first glance, it was readily obvious that the note contained two different sets of handwriting. One person had used pen, while the other had written in pencil. Some of the statements clearly were in response to others.

On one side, it said:

"From: Ta'varon
To: Priya"
with a big imperative, "Do not tell on body!" scrawled across the top. There were little hearts with faces next to the words, "kiss you! kiss me!"

On the other side, in pencil was:

"I'm sorry I called you ugly. I did not mean to say that. But I liked what you said on the note. I love you to. Your cute to. Do you want to be boyfriend and girlfriend? Yes or no give it back."

The user of the pen had then come along and circled the "Yes" and added:

"I love you to! I don't now about boyfriend and girlfriend and if you want to I don't care I like it to if you like it."

It was obvious to me that Ta'varon and Priya both contributed to the note, and that both of them need to learn the correct usage of the word "too." However, Priya's mom apparently is deeply concerned that her daughter is receiving notes not only from a boy, but from a boy with a split personality disorder.

No wonder she was so upset!

I didn't see the point of wasting any time in attempting to convince her that Priya had added to the note also, so I just told her I would talk to Ta'varon and take care of things. When she left, I called Romeo and Juliet out into the hall and showed them the note.

I first told Priya that I wasn't too impressed that she had lied to her mother about her involvement. She didn't even try to protest her innocence. Then I tried to convince both of them that they were WAY too young (TO young?) to be discussing love and relationships, and the school was no place for it anyway.

I was tempted to add, "If I don't even have a girlfriend, you shouldn't have one either!"

The love note must have been a hot topic of conversation in the lunchroom or on the playground, because I heard several kids whispering about who likes who while we were taking our bathroom break. Feeling the vibe, Isabel confided in me, "I have a crush on a boy."

Almost without thinking, I answered, "You know, a crush is something you should always keep secret and never tell anyone, especially a teacher."

I was just full of great romance advice today. But I wasn't the only one.

Not long after Isabel tried to tell me about her unrequited love, one of the Kindergarten teachers walked by. Thankfully, Katie waited until she was out of earshot before commenting, "There's a pretty lady for you to marry!"

Thanks, sweetheart! Can you look into what kind of a dowry I can expect to receive if I enter into a marriage contract with that lady? Get back to me on that, OK?

She said it so matter-of-factly, too, as if she was pointing out the only open seat in a crowded auditorium.

I suppose the good news is that whenever I'm ready to get back in the saddle again, I won't have to waste any hard-earned money on Match.com or eHarmony. Not when I've already got at my disposal a dogged little matchmaker AND a couple of experts in the art of writing love notes.

Talk to you later,

The Love Guru

Date:	Monday, March 29, 2010
To:	Fred Bommerson
From:	Jack Woodson
Subject:	It's all about the Abrahams, baby

Hey bud,

Ha! It sounds like the manager you've been dealing with is exactly like Priya's mother. Why is he refusing to believe that his own engineer had a hand in the latest proposal, and that it wasn't just you? Did you write, "kiss me! kiss you!" on the proposal?

Also, I'll see what I can do about getting Katie to find your soul mate. No guarantees, though, and it might cost you a crate of Capri Sun.

If today is any indication, this is going to be a very interesting week. My morning started with a little kid walking up to me and asking, "Is Abraham Lincoln dead?"

I answered, "Yep. And so are George Washington and Thomas Jefferson. Pretty much all of the money guys."

He then ran back to a slightly larger child and said, "Yeah, he's dead!"

I would love to have known what the lead-in on that conversation was, but unfortunately, I had to settle for that small piece of the puzzle. In my head, I imagine this is what preceded my involvement:

Big kid:	"One of the questions on my test last week asked who wrote the Declaration of Independence."
Little kid:	"That's easy – Uncle Sam!"
Big kid:	"No, I thought it was Bill somebody, but I picked Abraham Lincoln."
Little kid:	"I watched Transformers 2 last night, and Abraham Lincoln was in that!"
Big kid:	"No he wasn't. He died, like 10 years ago. Go ask that big guy."

Later, I moved from ancient history to current events. During our planning period, Mrs. Bird showed me some of the kids' recent work. She has been going over different writing styles, and last week was focused on newspaper articles. At the end of the week, she had the kids choose a topic and write a persuasive article along with a title and byline. There was "Give us more recess!" by Tyler, "No more dress code," by Smoker Anna, and "Free cupcakes every day," by Cerulean. The best title has to go to Clarisa, though, who had written an article requesting healthier food in the cafeteria. She titled her article "Eat some of this."

I got to talk to Clarisa later in the day, but it wasn't about her article. We had just come inside from the playground, and I was standing by the kids who were waiting in line to use the restroom. (Is it just me, or does the afternoon bathroom break seem to be a mystical vortex for funny stories?)

Clarisa and Betsy were both giggling and casting glances in my direction, so I asked what was up. I wondered if they had seen me at the Taco Bell again with someone else.

Betsy whispered something in Clarisa's ear, then Clarisa giggled again and said, "Jenny likes you."

Jenny is a little girl in Miss Palmerstein's class, and she's a little spitfire. I chose to play obtuse.

"Oh, really?" I replied. "I like her too. She's a very friendly third grader."

Betsy shook her head while Clarisa, with a puzzled look on her face, continued, "No, she doesn't like you as a teacher."

Barely withholding a grin, I responded, "She doesn't like me as a teacher? You mean she thinks I'm a bad teacher?"

At that, the girls exchanged looks, then Betsy clicked her tongue and declared, "He doesn't get it."

It was all I could do not to burst out laughing. I was already holding back giggles after seeing what was on the wall between the boys' and girls' restrooms.

Over the weekend, I had given my kids a chance for extra credit in science class. I asked them to take a piece of paper and make a poster about the importance of conserving our planet's resources.

My favorite was Lex's who had drawn some pictures of light bulbs and televisions and written, "Saving electricity is when you turn off everything that takes electricity and if you don't and go to church for five hours, the next day, you will get electric bill and you have to pay money. If you do turn off the lights and TV, you will not have to pay money."

Don't I wish!

But back to what was really making me laugh. Mrs. Bird had apparently gotten her hands on the poster that Shelly had made and decided to put it near the restrooms for all to see.

Shelly took something I had said last week very literally. Her poster had a big green triangle of arrows, like the universal recycling symbol. At the top corner of the triangle was a picture of a smiling child. At one of the bottom corners was a picture of a water fountain, and at the other corner was a picture of a toilet. Underneath all of this was the bold statement, "Mister Woodson told us that the water in the toilet is clean water when you flush the toilet it goes to a machine and it cleans the water so you can drink it."

The good news is that most of my kids don't pay any attention to things hanging on the wall, so I probably won't have to worry about kids actually drinking from the toilet. The bad news is that I might be getting some phone calls from parents regarding my teaching style.

At any rate, I think we can be thankful that Abraham Lincoln is not alive to see any misunderstanding that may arise from this poster. I can't be so sure about Bill somebody, though.
Later dude,

Mellow Yellow

Date: Wednesday, March 31, 2010
To: Fred Bommerson
From: Jack Woodson
Subject: Fighting and hurling and cussing, oh my!!

Hey buddy,

I'm holding you personally responsible for what I'm calling the Reverse Spam Bomb I received this morning. I've dubbed it Reverse Spam because instead of thousands of people getting the exact same email from a single source, I'm the one person who received the exact same email from multiple sources.

I got a one sentence message – "What's this I hear about you telling kids they can drink from the toilet?" – from Winter, Latya, Larry, Tiffany, and about ten others! Quite the coordinated effort you put into this, and I commend you. I should point out, though, that April Fool's Day is TOMORROW.

Not that my kids need some arbitrary date to act like fools. I have to wonder if it's possible to have a full moon in the middle of the afternoon. My kids were absolutely, off-the-wall INSANE today! No, no, I take that back. It actually started yesterday. At least the two third graders who had to go home suspended because they brought toy guns to school weren't in my class. But I was one of the teachers who had to confront them about it. Then, after school, just as they were about to get on the school buses and go home, two of my kids got into a fistfight.

My day today started with me dealing with these two wannabe pugilists. One of them, to absolutely no one's surprise, was Marshawn. I don't think this kid could walk by a cloister of nuns without provoking at least one of them to attack him. The other student, Franco, is certainly not my best behaved, but usually not prone to actual physical violence. However, according to all eyewitness accounts, the two of them were out there punching each other in the face. Franco, who is tall but scrawny, actually had the much larger Marshawn in a headlock, and was jabbing him in the nose. Marshawn, meanwhile, was pulling some sort of Matrix-like contortions, and reaching back over his shoulder to punch Franco.

As a result, they have both been suspended for the next three days, and we put them in different rooms for today. That brings us up to about 8:15 a.m. A wonderful time of the morning to regurgitate your breakfast all over the floor. At least that's what Kevin thought. Not really wanting a reenactment of the dinner scene from Monty Python's The Meaning of Life ("Better get a bucket"), I decided to take the rest of my class for a walk around the school while the custodian came to clean up the mess.

After lunch, I had a near-crisis on my hands when Ella told me that Lex had said "the S-word" to her. She looked positively shell-shocked, and I was already mentally gearing myself up to be angry with Lex. I figured that I ought to be sure of all the details first, though, so I asked Ella a few questions.

"What exactly did he say to you?" I asked.

"He pointed at us and laughed!" she declared. "Then he said the S-word!"

"What S-word? Can you whisper it to me? You won't be in trouble." I tried to reassure her, but at my request to hear the offensive term, Ella clamped both hands over her mouth and swiveled her head wildly.

"OK, then can you tell me what it rhymes with?" I expected her to say "bit," or "quit," or "barbecue pit," but I think my question merely confused her.

Then I had a flash of insight. I was suddenly able to view the situation from the perspective of a third grader, and I realized that what you and I automatically associate with "the S-word" might not be the case here.

"Did he call you stupid?" I asked, with my new awareness. Ella, still with hands clamped tightly over her mouth, nodded her head up and down vigorously.

Mystery solved, case closed.

I know that "stupid" is a derogatory word, but I do think Ella was reacting a bit in the extreme. Sure, I prosecuted Lex to the fullest extent of the law, but it's not like he yelled OUR "S-word" at her.

Having said that, I will admit that I have learned not to use the word "stupid" around the kids. Mainly because they do tend to treat it like a horrendous curse word. I always use the word "foolish" instead.

So as you can see, I've cleverly substituted the "F-word" for the "S-word."

My kids aren't the only ones acting out this week. At our after school meeting on Monday, I was sitting next to Mrs. Fitzgerald in the cafeteria when she directed my attention to a box of supplies sitting over in the corner. She said, "Look at that box, and see if you can guess what my kids were calling each other today."

I scanned the printing on the box – "Napkins, cups, black sporks, trays."

Would you believe I guessed correctly? Her kids were calling each other black sporks!! These kids will grab at anything to put each other down!

We spent the rest of the meeting coming up with our own list of things the kids could call each other to REALLY burn.

Yellow Highlighter
Late Homework
Sticky Note
Dirty Overhead Transparency
Outlying Data
Adopted Curriculum

I think being called any of these things would be a major blow to the ego, but I guess none of them even come close to calling someone a spork.

OH SNAP!!

Talk to you later,

Stu Pidass

Date: Thursday, April 8, 2010
To: Fred Bommerson
From: Jack Woodson
Subject: Whack-a-mole

Hey Fred,

Apparently my list of nasty words for third graders either touched a nerve or got some creative juices flowing, because I've received several emails from your esteemed colleagues calling me names. Winter called me a Defective Widget. Larry insinuated that I was a Cracked Ceramic. Tiffany said I had Worn Out Tooling.

It's ok, though. My feelings weren't hurt. I just called them all Big Fat Solder Blobs.

Once more, my classroom has become the revolving door. My latest ward, Marshawn, has left our fine school for better and brighter things. After returning from suspension on Tuesday, he was right back to his usual tricks – cussing at other kids, spouting non-sense, and sleeping in class. He had saved his craziest bon mots for Mrs. Bird, though. See if you can guess which one of these statements Marshawn did NOT share with Mrs. Bird and her class over the past couple of days:

A)   "My dad is in jail!"
B)   "My granny hit her head on a log and died, and
            her body is in the closet!"
C)   "My mom puts Benadryl in my juice!"
D)   "My family appreciates kind gestures, floral-
            scented potpourri, and breakfast in bed!"

If you said anything other than D, you are a Corroded Wingnut.

I'm sure Marshawn will be all right, though. After all, there are kids everywhere for him to call fat asses and no shortage of toilets to go berserk on. In much sadder news, I also lost another student yesterday, and she was one of my favorites. Tiny Anna, who is a very friendly and bright girl, brought in withdrawal papers yesterday. At first, I told her I wouldn't sign them, but of course I had no choice. Her family is moving to Lancaster, which isn't all that far from here, but it's far enough to put her in another school. Maybe once she gets to her new school, her mother will allow her to obtain a pair of forbidden glasses.

Losing a sweetheart stinks, but losing a maniac isn't too bad. However, Marshawn's replacement, who arrived yesterday, makes Marshawn look like an upright, responsible member of society.

This new kid showed up with his father around 1:00 yesterday. He literally looked like something the cat had dragged in. He had on a T-shirt that looked like it had been turned inside out, his whole face looked filthy, and the whites of his eyes were much more yellowish than white.

His name is Marcus, and the first things out of his father's mouth were that Marcus is a troublemaker, he got suspended at his old school a lot, and that "he might try to run away from you."

Great! So now I'm what, Agent Girard from The Fugitive??

"What I need from each and every one of you teachers is a hard target search of every classroom, break room, bathroom, book room, and store room within a 10 mile radius."

Marcus didn't try to run away today, but he certainly did get under my nerves. For a kid who's four-foot-nothing, he's got more attitude than a Jersey Shore cast member. Some teachers are able to ignore disrespect and rudeness and move on, but I've always been stubborn. I have a real problem with little kids who ignore me and/or talk back.

My mood was worsened at around 2:30 today. I had pulled my new friend out into the hallway to have a chat. He had written a really nasty note in his math journal and was flashing it at all the kids around him. I thought it would be helpful to point out a few things to him.

1) The math journals are for – surprise! – math problems and not for starting fights.

2) I have 20/20 vision and can thus see everything he does in class.

3) There are better strategies to make friends at a new school than writing threatening notes.

4) The word "kill" (in his note, several times) has TWO L's.

I didn't seem to be getting through to Marcus, judging by the way he was rolling his eyes and over-sighing. Then Roy'al, from Mrs. Frisch's class, walked by. I don't know exactly why he was out in the hallway or where he was going. He might have been going to the special ed portable. He might have been delivering a message to the office. He might have been on his way to set a fire in the custodian's closet.

What I do know is that as he walked by me, he was muttering obscenities JUST loudly enough to be sure I heard them. What a prince.

I called out to him to come back to where I was, but he kept walking. I raised my voice and told him to stop, but he kept walking. I pulled out my magic wand, pointed it at him, and shouted, "PETRIFICUS TOTALUS!!" All to no avail.

(Just so you know, the Extreme Fundamentalist Christians have got it all wrong – Harry Potter does NOT in fact teach you how to cast spells.)

I suppose if there's any good news to this story, it's that Marcus gained a new role model today, someone he can admire and emulate. And no, I'm not talking about me.

I wrote a referral on Roy'al, and he'll be suspended on Monday and Tuesday. I also grabbed a stack of referrals to have on hand, because I foresee needing plenty more before the year is out.

Benadryl in the juice, eh? That's something to consider.
Talk to you later,

Unhappy Gilmore

Date: Tuesday, April 13, 2010
To: Fred Bommerson
From: Jack Woodson
Subject: It's not rocket surgery!

Hey Fred,

Easy for you to say that you'll miss Marshawn, since you never had to deal with him. The kid was only present in my class for fourteen days, but it seemed like two years!

Marcus may prove to be much worse, especially if he starts following Roy'al's lead. By the way, I think you're right. Next time I need to get Roy'al to stop and listen, I'll shout, "Look! Defenseless kittens!" That should get his attention.

At least I have one thing in my favor in terms of the new kid. Marcus is apparently the smart one in his family. He has two first grade sisters – twins – in Miss Phelps' class, and she says neither of them can even write their own name.

I can't devote all my energy to Marcus right now, because with the TAKS test fast approaching, I am banging my head against the wall with some of the other children. I still have kids subtracting 10 and 4 and getting 14. I still have kids that think their pencil is 8 miles long. I still have kids adding a dollar and a nickel and getting 6 cents. Or sometimes 6 dollars.

Not only do their actions not make sense, but sometimes their words don't even make sense! Franco encountered a problem this afternoon and blurted out, "Man, that's hard! That's harder than a turtle!"

I wanted to reply, "No way, it's easy! It's easier than elevator music!" Instead, I let the mixed metaphor slide.

Victor still can't remember his shape names. I quizzed him today, and he couldn't tell me the name of an 8-sided figure. I tried to give him a hint – "What's the animal that lives in the ocean and has eight legs?"

Without any hesitation, Victor nodded, looked me in the eyes, and answered confidently, "A squid."

NO!! Well, I mean, technically, yes, he gave a correct answer to that question, but NO!! There's no such thing as a squidagon!!

I'm at that point where some teachers might just throw in the towel and show movies all day. I'll admit, I've thought about it.

Maybe a continuous loop of "The Lion King 3 7/8: Simba Swallows His Pride."

But I'm not a quitter. I'm not a giver-upper. I AM willing to modify my techniques. Therefore, I have decided that I shall henceforth teach in the style of Mr. Noodle, from Elmo's World.

My nephew Kyle is a HUGE fan of Elmo and Mr. Noodle. They're both relatively new additions to Sesame Street, so I don't think they were around when your son was that age. I should probably explain what I'm talking about.

Mr. Noodle is a character that (seemingly) lives in Elmo's window and has a very unique style of interpreting questions. Allow me to give you an example.

Elmo will roll up the shade, "waking" Mr. Noodle (the similarities to a peep show booth stop, for the most part, there). Elmo will then ask Mr. Noodle about whatever the topic of the day is. Swimming, cows, badgies, whatever. If the topic of the day is footwear, Elmo may say, "Mr. Noodle, how do you put on your shoes?"

Mr. Noodle will then do something outrageously stupid like putting a shoe in his mouth, making Elmo wonder if he has an IQ below 30.

At this point, a group of unseen kids will join the fray, shouting from off camera, "NOOOOO, that's not right, Mr. Noodle!!"

The Noodle will then do something only slightly less "touched," such as putting the shoes down his pants. Again, the kids will patiently yell, "NOOOOO, Mr. Noodle! Shoes don't go there!"

Typically, Mr. Noodle will perform a third troglodytic act, maybe balancing a shoe on his head. At this point, we're all waiting to hear the kids shout, "Are you EFFING SH!TTING me???" but they always seem to be inhumanly restrained.

Elmo himself will ultimately have to demonstrate the correct way to put on shoes.

That's enough of the Wikipedia article about Elmo's World. The point I'm getting at is that I am going to reverse my whole teaching style and try to Noodle it up a bit more. No more probing questions for accurate answers. Instead, when we talk about perimeter, I'm going to randomly make tally marks then wait for the kids to realize that I'm doing the wrong thing and shout, "NOOOOO!" at me. Then I'll start dividing a circle into wedges until they shout at me again.

Maybe I will have more success with this technique than ever before.

I read an article the other day about how schools across the country are taking one move towards Noodlehood. They've gotten it in their collective heads that a great way to start making fiscal cuts is to do away with school libraries.

Your first thought may be, "But where will Colonel Mustard kill Mr. Boddy with the Lead Pipe?" Don't worry, the article didn't say anything about budget cuts to Billiard Rooms.

Let's just remove a giant resource and wealth of literature from children in their formative years. Sounds like a plan worthy of Mr. Noodle, indeed.

Now I'm going to send this email by touching my monitor with my nose. If that doesn't work, I'll turn around three times in my swivel chair and hoot like an owl.

Later,

Dumb Perignon

Date: Friday, April 16, 2010
To: Fred Bommerson
From: Jack Woodson
Subject: The Clash of the Cretins

Hey buddy,

It is indeed a great time to travel. I'm sure Boston in April is fantastic. Not that you'll get to see a whole heck of a lot of it next week, stuck in customer meetings. I would advise you to refrain from channeling Mr. Noodle during any of those meetings. I have to admit, though, I did snort at your line about licking a heat pump if anyone asked how it works.

Can you ask Paul if he can spring for an extra ticket so I can go to Boston with you guys? There are a few kids here that I could really stand to get away from for a few days, weeks, or lifetimes.

My newest charge, Marcus, is not doing much to endear himself to me. He is blatantly disrespectful, he lies, and I think he may be withholding information about Jimmy Hoffa's whereabouts.

As we switched classes today, I was standing by my door greeting the students, and I couldn't help but notice the top of Marcus's head. He's about half my height, so I had no problem getting a full view of his noggin. He's got really short hair to begin with, not quite shaved but almost, and carved into what little hair there was, right on the top of the sphere, were the letters J.D.

Please keep in mind that this kid's name starts with an M, which is neither a J nor a D. When I asked him who had written on top of his head, he immediately replied, "Nobody."

Not believing for an instant that his hair naturally grows like that, I tried to press him for more information, but, as usual, he wouldn't tell me anything. Mrs. Bird had a little more luck later in the day. She told me that when she had asked Marcus about his newest 'do, he told her that a friend had done it to display his nickname.

Here I thought he was selling out his melon as a JD Powers billboard. But no, it was intended to be DJ, not JD. The boy's self-appointed nickname is "DJ Cool."

In my opinion, DJ Dyslexic would be more like it.

Later, I had to leave a message with Marcus' father about a little outburst he had right after recess.

On most days, I let the kids enter my classroom as soon as they are done using the restroom, rather than waiting until the entire class is done. That way, they get a little more time to work on the word problem that day. Except for the stragglers like Cerulean, who always takes about fifteen minutes to use the bathroom. Which I encourage her to do. Of course.

On Fridays, though, the kids don't do a word problem since they have tests to take, so instead of having them enter the classroom, I told the first couple of kids to just line up in the hallway outside my room.

By the time Marcus came out of the restroom, there were already about eight or nine kids sitting quietly in line by my door. Mrs. Bird was down at that end of the hall near our classrooms, and I was monitoring the bathrooms at the other end. A moment later, Marcus came running back to ask me, "Do we go in the room?"

I looked around the corner and pointed out the kids sitting in the hallway. "Don't you see the line down there?" I asked him. "You need to be in that line."

Five or six minutes later, when the last child was done, I rounded the corner to rejoin my class. But the line was gone. Mrs. Bird was there with her class, but my door was open and my kids were inside. Furthermore, the overhead machine was on, and the science test was being displayed.

I asked Mrs. Bird why the kids had gone inside, and she looked surprised and said that Marcus had told her that I had told him to lead the class in. He had told her that I had instructed him to, "Go in and cut the overhead on."

She added that it didn't really sound like something I would say, but that he had insisted.

I called him out into the hallway for questioning. Amazingly, he stuck with his story, including my odd choice of words.

It's one thing to be caught in a white lie. But to stand there face-to-face (or in our case, face-to-belt-buckle) and actually be angry that I was contradicting his story is quite another thing. He got so mad, in fact, that at one point, he stormed back to his desk, screaming the whole way. Not a scream with words, just a primal blast that rose in pitch. Mrs. Bird and I exchanged glances that clearly said, "What the –??!?" Most of the kids in the room had a similar expression.

That's when I made the phone call and left a message with his dad. Then he and I had another conversation in the hall. When I mentioned the screaming, he immediately rebuffed me. "I didn't scream!"

"Yes, when you went back to your desk, you were screaming. Everyone heard you."

Marcus rolled his eyes and asked, in an incredibly sarcastic tone, "Really? Everyone??"

As he stared defiantly at me, I practiced my deep breathing techniques. Finally, when my teeth unclenched, I stated again, "I don't appreciate your screaming when I'm trying to talk to you."

Again, he claimed, "I wasn't screaming!"

"What do you call what you were doing then?" I asked him.

"I was yelling."

I must have stared at him for two full minutes while my brain filtered through a myriad of things I couldn't say, couldn't do, shouldn't even be thinking. I had to bite down on my tongue, hard, not to call him a spork. Eventually, what came out was, "I'm looking forward to hearing back from your father."

On top of this little thorn in my side, I have a new student in the same class as of yesterday. This little girl, Gloria, has been at the school all year long and has been a real headache for two of the other third grade teachers. Last week, she upped the ante a bit, throwing a crayon at Mrs. Frisch and punching Mrs. Fitzgerald in the arm. That's right, she punched a teacher. After three days of suspension, she returned to school, displaced into another third-grade classroom. I guess Mrs. Forest felt Mrs. Bird and I would not mind dodging crayons or being punched repeatedly.

Gloria was relatively well behaved for both of us yesterday, and she didn't have any major flare-ups today, but I've had interactions with this girl before, and I know her temperament. The worst part is that she seems to have developed a real bond with DJ Clueless. Maybe it's the head inscription, maybe it's the disregard for rules, maybe it's the complete illiteracy. Whatever the reason, they're tight.

Lord help us all.

Seriously, I'm going to be checking my email all weekend for permission to go to Boston with you.

Later,

Jimmy Outtaheer

Hey bud,

Yeah, I didn't really think Paul would come through with an extra ticket. And your point is absolutely valid – these kids probably WOULD kill a substitute in my absence. I just can't have that on my conscience.

So how's the trip? Have you been able to shave P.R. into Ron Philby's hair yet? That would make for some interesting discussions around the table at your plant visits.

Well, while you're having a blast touring New England, I can't dodge the fact that the TAKS test is next week! This is most likely the reason my heart is pounding, I can't feel my toes, and my stomach feels like a troop of armored butterflies has taken up permanent residence.

I can't help but notice that an uncomfortably large number of my students are still filling in bubbles very carelessly and sloppily on multiple choice tests. They know that they need to neatly fill in one bubble for each question, yet some of them turn in tests where their answer choices look like they were made while having an epileptic seizure during an earthquake.

It occurred to me that the kids might not know that a machine would be scoring their tests. A heartless, soulless machine that won't care if all of the correct steps were followed to find the answer; only that the correct bubble was filled in neatly and completely.

Skynet's most ruthless creation wasn't the killer cyborg Terminators. It was the test-grading machines in Austin, Texas.

Before telling them about this, I asked the kids who THEY thought would be grading their tests. This made for a very interesting give-and-take.

Me:	"Who do you think is going to grade your TAKS tests?"
Ava:	"The teacher?"
Me:	"Nope."
Mickey:	"You?"
Me:	"Uh, I AM the teacher, so STILL no."

Big Jack:	"Mrs. Bird?"
Me:	"Seriously??"
Tyler:	"No, she IS the teacher, so still NO!"
Mia:	"You a GOOD teacher!"
Me:	"OK, thanks, but let's get this back to the question."
DaQuayvius:	"The principal?"
Me:	"No."
Temperance:	"The President?"

None of the kids knew that it wouldn't be a person grading their tests, and one actually thought President Barrack Obama would be taking time out of his busy schedule to pick up a red pen and score thousands of TAKS! Forget the mess of our economy, never mind the whole international politics scene – give the guy a key to the 3rd grade math test, and put him to work!

The kids were stunned to discover that a machine would be grading their tests. A few equated "machine" to "robot" and asked if it had a name. I told them it was "Grady McSparksalot." I can only hope that this translates into neater, cleaner bubbling.

After our discussion, we got back into review mode. This whole week is devoted to reviewing everything we've covered so far this year. We began this morning with some quick hits on weight and measurement. Weight is such an abstract concept for the kids. They know that anything heavier than a car should be measured in tons and that anything lighter than a loaf of bread should be measured in ounces. But in between those two benchmarks, there is a vast abyss of confusion.

When I told them that I weigh 200 pounds, there was a class-wide reaction that suggested they thought I was heavier than a whale. In an effort to show that heavy does not necessarily mean morbidly obese, I brought up Shaquille O'Neal, who weighs close to 300 pounds.

Lance only heard the first syllable of the name and looked excitedly around the room as he purred, "Oooooh, Shakira! I LIKE Shakira!!"

I like your thinking, kid, but c'mon, let's try to focus, OK?

Moving on to capacity, when I asked the kids how many quarts were in a gallon, most of them remembered! More than a few even shouted, "May the quarts be with you!"

YES!!

Knowing that one of my mnemonics had worked, I was emboldened to try another. This time, I had one for symmetry (or cemetery, as my kids say).

First I asked who liked the movie Toy Story. Unsurprisingly, everyone raised their hands (including me). Then I double checked to make sure that they knew who Buzz Lightyear was. They did.

Finally I said, "Now remember that part in the movie where he shouts 'To the SYMMETRY and beyond!' And then he hits the little red button on his chest, and his wings pop up, exactly the same on both sides, just like he has a line of symmetry!"

Naturally, the kids' first reaction was to argue with me – "THAT'S not what he says!!!"

Still, they thought it was pretty funny, and I heard several kids repeat it a few times throughout the class period.

During recess, I asked a couple of the kids to show Mrs. Bird our new way of remembering symmetry, and nearly every one of them proudly shouted, "May the fourths be with you!"

Pass the Tylenol.

I guess I can use this in tomorrow's review of fractions – ½ of our silly memory devices have been retained!

I'll talk to you later,

Buzz Slightfear

Date: Thursday, April 22, 2010
To: Fred Bommerson
From: Jack Woodson
Subject: Drillin' like a villain

Hey man,

Listen man, "trying too hard" is a prerequisite for this job. Have I taught you nothing? Funny, those last five words are what I often find myself muttering to the kids as well.

Given the choice of meeting President Obama or Shakira, you know I would make the same choice as you. And she does NOT weigh 300 pounds. Since you're up in Boston, you probably won't meet Shakira, but you might run into Shaq. If you do, be sure to greet him with, "May the fourths be with you!"

Mrs. Forest sent out an email today that included "The Starfish Story," where this couple sees a guy throwing starfish back into the ocean. The beach is littered with starfish, so the couple remark to the guy that he can't possibly make a difference because there are so many starfish. The guy then looks at the one currently in his hand and says, "I can make a difference to THIS one!" as he throws it back into the ocean.

Mrs. Forest sent this to us hoping to lift our spirits during this stressful time and to let us know that we CAN make a difference. It inspires me with a desire to throw a few of my students into the ocean.

It's probably a good thing we don't live anywhere near the water.

My day had an interesting little wrinkle in it, and I hope it's something that DID make a difference for my kids. At around 10:30, Mr. Redd stuck his head into my room and knocked lightly on the door. When I looked up from what I was doing, he motioned me over and softly said, "I need to tell you something."

Of course, as soon as Mr. Redd first disturbed the air molecules in the doorway, the kids had totally lost interest in what they were doing and were staring at him. Throughout the year, we have gone over the visitor procedure many, many times. When a visitor walks into the room, the kids are supposed to completely ignore the visitor and continue doing whatever it was they were already doing. Only if that visitor specifically talks to them are they to pay any attention to that person.

In practice, the complete opposite happens. When somebody walks into the room, the kids all swivel around in their chairs and stare the person down. This happens more often per day than you might think. I have a lot of kids coming and going to and from various tutoring groups throughout the day, and when they leave my class or come back into my class, I never have the full attention of my kids. Same goes for when another teacher walks in to talk to me. It is incredibly aggravating.

Anyway, I walked over to the door to conference with Mr. Redd, who looked much more serious than he usually does. He started with, "Don't tell anybody this. I probably shouldn't even be saying anything."

My eyes darted sideways, and I could see that every child in the room was listening with bated breath, waiting to hear the gossip that Mr. Redd shouldn't be sharing. You could hear a mechanical pencil lead drop.

Mr. Redd went on, "When you see the words 'How many more' in a word problem, it means you're comparing two things and you're supposed to subtract."

I stroked my chin thoughtfully as I fake-pondered the importance of his words and as the two of us did our best not to ruin the moment by laughing. We had come up with this plan a few weeks ago while commiserating with each other at happy hour, er, I mean, at book study one evening.

I do my best to impart pearls of wisdom to the kids every day, but too many of them choose not to listen. Yet, like I said before, when the kids SHOULD be ignoring a visitor and focusing on their work, they instead listen raptly to the conversation with the visitor. Maybe gaining the knowledge through eavesdropping on Mr. Redd will last longer. Who knows? I need to return the favor in HIS class, and I'm thinking about whispering, "Did you know that TAKS really stands for 'Texas Accentuates Kids' Suffering?'"

There is still the problem of the complete loss of production any time somebody walks into the classroom, though. I am very tempted to start running visitor drills. Grading the kids on their response or lack of response to people entering the room. Why not? It's not like we don't do enough drills at this school.

In fact, the powers that be have for some reason decided to cram all of this month's required drills into this week. We had a fire drill on Monday and a crisis drill yesterday. That's a bit much. Especially when you add in all the drills I already make the kids do when I get irritated with them.

"All right, that's the FOURTH time you've told me three plus four equals nine! Drop and give me twenty!"

After school yesterday, Miss Palmerstein told me that she had heard from Ms. Zapata that we were due a tornado drill. That's one we don't do very often, where we have to take the kids out into the hallway and have them kneel down in front of the wall.

All day long, I was prepped for the tornado drill. So when it finally came at 2:15, I was the first teacher out the door in the 3rd grade hallway. I already had five or six kids ducking and covering when Mrs. Bird's class started to pour out from across the hallway. Fortunately, only two more kids had assumed the position before Mrs. Bird pointed out that we were having another fire drill, NOT a tornado drill.

Hey, my kids might have burned, but at least they wouldn't be harmed by falling debris.

Chalk up my mistake to the stress I'm feeling over the TAKS next Tuesday. My left eyeball is twitching more than a frog's legs under an applied electric current. Eyeballs are pretty much not supposed to do that. But some of my kids still don't seem anywhere close to ready.

Today in tutoring, I asked Suzie how many minutes were in one hour. She just stared at me with a blank expression. I asked her to turn her attention to the clock hanging on the wall, and to count by fives all the way around the clock. She counted 5, 10, 15... all the way up to 60. Perfect. Then I asked her again how many minutes were in one hour. She thought about it for a few seconds, and then replied, "One?"

Now, not only is my eyeball in danger, but my forehead has a huge red welt from me pounding it against the wall.

At this point, I have to believe that my kids either have the knowledge or they don't. Cramming is probably not going to make a difference. Maybe it's time to start chucking starfish.
Later,

Teddy Ornott

Date: Tuesday, April 27, 2010
To: Fred Bommerson
From: Jack Woodson
Subject: Panic A-TAKS

Hey man,

I told you that eavesdropping strategy works wonders! I'm glad you and Winter were able to put it to good use to once and for all end Larry's weekly demand for Arby's.

I've had a super long week, and it's only Tuesday! These past two days have been the longest of the year. Either I've fallen into my own personal version of Groundhog Day, or it's TAKS week.

Time to see if I've made an impact in any of these kids' brains. Like I mentioned last time, I reached a point late last week where I just had to accept that if they don't know it by now, they're not going to know it for the test. As one of my old college professors used to say, "Time for me to let go of your hand and see if you walk out in front of a truck."

Ironically, that same professor was himself severely injured when a truck fell on top of him during a Force and Load demonstration gone horribly wrong.

Typically, kids do bring their A-game to the table on test day, and quite often, kids who don't seem to know their head from a hole in the ground will do well. It's just that I have a sinking suspicion that several kids in my group this year would need to undergo some sort of "Flowers for Algernon" process in order to pull off a miracle like that.

I did all I could do to motivate and bribe. I told the kids that everyone who did their best would get to have a reward pizza and movie party on Friday. I promised extra blue tickets to everyone who spent time checking their work. I told Antonio that I had plenty more coupons for free meals at the Golden Corral if he put his best effort into it.

Grudgingly, I had to comply with the state-mandated directive of covering everything in my room. Anything that contains print or numbers must be covered up. Last Friday, I had to spend about an hour stapling butcher paper to my walls to cover up bulletin boards, the word wall, the number line, and just about everything else that was too big or too high to take down. You know, I can understand the need to remove posters, signs, and boards that contain mathematically-related items, but some of this is just downright silly! I have an alphabet strip running the length of the wall above my whiteboard, and I had to cover up the letters! I'm so sure that a student is going to be immersed in the TAKS, look up at those letters, and in a flash of insight, suddenly comprehend the answer to the question he was stuck on for 20 minutes.

"Thank you, Cursive P! You saved my bacon once again!"

Since they don't let us monitor our own kids anymore – after all, the word "teachers" CAN be rearranged to spell the word "cheaters" – I was up in Mrs. Jones' 5th grade classroom while she was in mine. This made for two very long days of doing nothing but walking around the room, keeping the kids quiet and focused on their tests. Oh, and replacing broken and dull pencils. Because as soon as one kid asks for a new pencil, twenty others need one too.

During the test, we're not allowed to say anything to the kids that could be construed as help or hints. We are trained to respond to any requests for help with one universal mantra.

Student:	"How do you say this word?"
Teacher:	"Just do your best."
Student:	"I don't understand this question."
Teacher:	"Just do your best."
Student:	"I fell out of my chair and landed on my pencil, and now I'm bleeding profusely from the ear!"
Teacher:	"Just do your best."

It's pretty easy for the first two hours or so, when the kids are still answering the questions. It's when they finish the last question that the squirrelly behavior starts to come out.

They all know that they're supposed to go back and check their work and find mistakes. Most of them have been told that it would not be the best decision to even think about turning their test in before lunch. So as a compromise, most of them will spend hours pretending to check their work. This can be amusing to the observing teacher for a few seconds, but it gets old quickly when the child keeps looking back every few seconds to see if you're noticing that they are checking.

"Yes, student who so desperately wants me to think that you are actually checking your work, I DO see you deliberately counting on your fingers! Way to go!!"

Aside from that, Mrs. Jones' class was pretty well behaved and did their business. My class wasn't quite so accommodating.

Mrs. Jones caught me after school today to tell me that Suzie had fallen asleep twice before lunch, that Eddie had finished his test and then loudly announced to the class, "I'M FINISHED!" and that Shelly had basically just played with her hair and nails all day long.

On a positive note, Mrs. Jones mentioned that several times during the math test, she heard kids muttering, "Use the force." I told her I had taught them a Jedi mind trick. I wanted to follow up with, "I have the death sentence in twelve systems!" but I didn't want to confuse her any further.

Over in Mrs. Bird's class, there was one case of idiocy. During the reading test yesterday, Gwenn actually tore out a piece of her test booklet so she could write a note to the girl in front of her! Mr. Utoobay, who was monitoring that class, handed me the torn out piece and said, "Maybe she thought she'd get a head start on the 4th grade writing TAKS." Gwenn's note consisted of one word – "Hola!"

I'm sorry, but if you're going to go to the ridiculous extreme of MUTILATING the document that determines whether or not you go to the next grade, you had damn well better write something more than, "Hola!" I'd better see Paul's Letter to the Ephesians or the complete lyrics to "American Pie."

Joaqim and Marcus turned their tests in before nine-thirty. For those of you keeping track at home, you can just write those two off right now.

I will be having several lengthy discussions with students tomorrow. But the good news is that standardized testing is over for another year. Now we have to play the waiting game for the results. I'd much rather be playing Stratego or Hungry Hungry Hippo.

Later,

Walker, TAKSes Ranger

I took Lex down to Ms. Zapata's office and explained the phone call I had just had. Ms. Zapata was not impressed with Lex OR his mother. She said that Lex would be suspended AT HOME next week.

Poor Lex. Three days of watching cartons and eating ice cream. And possibly working on actually connecting with his punches.

Crap, I probably SHOULD have put him in a first grade classroom. Next time, and I'm sure there will be a next time, I'll suspend him in-school. Let it never be said that I don't learn from my mistakes.

And when Lex comes back on Thursday, I'll be sure to tell him not to curse, not to tattle, not to pretend to be blind, not to stick toothpicks in his butt, and so on, and so on. I'd better start making a list now.

Later,

Mel O'Drama

Date: Monday, May 3, 2010
To: Fred Bommerson
From: Jack Woodson
Subject: Alas, poor Pluto, we knew you well

Hey dude,

No, Lex's mom will most likely NOT be adding me to her email list and forwarding funny videos. That's a very astute observation. I'm guessing she would never go out of her way to help me change a flat tire, either.

Thanks for letting me vent in that last email. Today's tone will be noticeably more breezier, I promise.

Right off the bat, one thing that's breezier is my now tie-free attire, as the summer dress code is back in effect. We got an email last week that covered "Acceptable and Unacceptable Dress," and I found a few of the bullet points quite humorous.

For one thing, the memo specifically banned bib overalls from being worn at schools. This makes me wonder two things: Who actually necessitated that clause by showing up to school in bib overalls, and did they also have a hayseed sticking between their two front teeth?

Also, Spandex has been outlawed. I'm OK with this, because I already wear Spandex at night to fight crime (and to rock out with super-crazy dance moves), so I don't need to wear it at school, too.

This morning, as I walked Spandex-free around the classroom observing the kids doing their morning work, I noticed an overpoweringly sweet smell coming from one table. It seemed to be coming from Jessie's area, so I stopped to talk with him. Here's how the conversation went:

Me:	"Is somebody over here wearing perfume or cologne?"
Jessie:	"No."
Me:	"Really?"
Jessie:	"Yes."
Me:	"OK. How many times did you push the spray button?"
Jessie:	"One."
Me:	"Smells like more than one."
Jessie:	"Five."

I don't think most people realize that teachers often have to be master detectives and interrogators to get to the bottom of things. Not to mention expert handwriting analysts to figure out who didn't put their name on a test or who forged their parent's signature on their report card.

With TAKS behind us, and only about a month left in the school year, we can finally get around to some of the fun stuff on the curriculum. Today we started to read about the solar system from our science textbooks. These are the same textbooks we've been using since I started teaching, so they are a bit outdated in terms of the current planetary lineup.

When we came across the sentence that said, "There are nine planets in the solar system, including Earth," I had to stop for a moment and explain why this was no longer the case.

All of the kids seemed dumbfounded that Pluto was no longer considered a planet. Mickey even blurted out, "Pluto got blowed up?"

No, it was more like being voted off the island. Maybe I should tell the kids that there was one big episode of Solar System Idol, and Pluto's performance just wasn't up to snuff. Some experts questioned its choice of "Cold as Ice" by Foreigner, and the gold sequined unitard really had people wondering.

Here's what the judges had to say:

Randy: "You rock, dawg! Really! You're a rock, and
           you're named after a Disney dawg!"

Simon: "That was really pathetic. You call yourself a
           planet – but where's the warmth? I've seen
           more personality and spirit from an errant
           comet. Next you'll be claiming planethood for
           that so-called 'moon' of yours."

Paula: "Our mystic fathers joined together to drink
           from the river of the galaxy. I feel like the
           ultimate bingo winner in a high stakes universe
           with multiple realities. Meet me in my dressing
           room."

Ultimately a big group of scientists banded together to kick Pluto to the curb. I think I read somewhere that Mel Gibson's father has already begun to promote the word that there have always only been eight planets.

I told the kids that one of the reasons for Pluto's exile was that it did not meet size requirements. It was just too small to be a planet.

Clarisa asked me, "So Pluto is so small it would fit in this room?"

Um, noooo, not quite THAT small.

"But it would fit inside the school, right?"

To them, small means a cat, and big means an elephant. Anything beyond that, and they have a very hard time comprehending. Telling them Pluto is small is kind of like telling them that a Pinot Noir from 1857 is overrated – they're just not going to grasp it.

Interestingly enough, Uranus is still large enough to be considered a planet.

Later,

Mel Keyway

Date: Wednesday, May 5, 2010
To: Fred Bommerson
From: Jack Woodson
Subject: Bad Breath of a Salesman

Hey man,

Nope, I don't think Uranus humor will ever not be funny. I've entertained myself greatly over the past couple of days by slipping Uranus jokes into conversation during science class. At last count, I was up to 19.

In fact, Mrs. Davidson, the Behavioral Unit teacher who's been sitting in class with Felicia, had to excuse herself from the room yesterday because she started giggling loudly. This left us with a potentially dangerous situation, because I don't think Felicia's pepper water would stand a chance against the denizens of Uranus.

20!

Yesterday, we went to an assembly in the auditorium so the kids could learn about this year's fundraising activity. Each child was given a case of "World's Greatest Chocolate" bars to sell to their friends and family (and weak-willed teachers), and sales will benefit the PTA at the school.

The guy who gave the presentation kept the kids' attention by doing a lot of magic tricks and promising great prizes to anyone who sold a lot of chocolate. Mention prizes to these kids and they go bananas. They have no intention whatsoever of actually doing whatever it takes to WIN the prizes, but just HEARING about the prizes is like winning the lottery for them.

They've been doing the candy bar sales here at my school for several years now. Before that, it was some kind of coupon book they had to sell.

This makes me think back to when I was in the third grade, and my school's fundraiser was having us sell fertilizer door-to-door. I didn't think anything of it at the time, but looking back on it, that seems a really odd choice of merchandise to have an eight-year-old child sell. But sell it, I did. I sold more than anyone else in my class. I don't know if this was because people in my neighborhood really needed fertilizer, or if it was just a welcome relief from all of the other kids selling candy.

"If that's just another snot-nosed kid selling M&M's... Wait – what's this? Fertilizer?!? THANK YOU, GOD!!"

I remember there was one guy in the neighborhood who really boosted my sales. The whole time I was meticulously working my way through my carefully prepared sales pitch, he was making impatient gestures as if to say, "Get on with it," and when I finally did finish, he immediately stated, "Yeah, okay, gimme twenty bags."

I can understand buying a two dollar candy bar because you want the kid doing the hard sell to feel successful. Nobody pity-buys a fifty-pound bag of fertilizer.

Thankfully, I wasn't out there lugging around huge bags of manure – it was a system of pre-order and cash on delivery. And instead of some crappy plastic prizes like my students get here at the school, we were actually paid a commission. For every bag we sold, we received a Susan B. Anthony dollar. When I first laid eyes on this previously unheard of coinage – the reward for my hard efforts – my reaction was, "What the *%$# is that??"

But, ridiculous coinage aside, I had been paid handsomely for my hard work, so I offered to use some of my money to take the family out to dinner. We went to Pizza Hut and pigged out. When my mom and I went up to the counter to pay at the end of the meal, I carefully laid out ten Susies before the waitress got to the register. When she came to ring us up, she asked, "Who put all these quarters here?"

My current third graders don't need to worry about being paid in some obscure monetary unit. Instead, the kids who sell at least two boxes will get a little party at the end of the school year with an air bounce, ring toss, and other hokey little games.

They'd probably just lose the quarters anyway.

Personally, I think it's rather foolish to give every kid a case of candy bars right off the bat. Not all of them are going to have the drive to sell them and return with money. Or, in the case of Cerulean, they might not have the will power not to just eat the chocolate themselves.

Cerulean, who walks herself from Ms. Hamm's special ed class back to my room around 2:45 each afternoon, decided today to duck into the bathroom and eat herself into a chocolate-induced stupor.

Someone found her in the back corner of the restroom, glassy-eyed and near-comatose. Talk about a Functional Voiding Disturbance! She had eaten five candy bars and unwrapped a sixth. No amount of magic tricks can counter that sort of determination.

On a completely different note, Jill called me last night. I almost didn't answer the phone, but I'm really glad I did. We talked for quite a while, and the key message was that she wants to get back together. She said that she went out with the ex-boyfriend a couple of times and quickly realized that the spark wasn't there and that she missed me. She wanted to wait until after the stress of TAKS to contact me, but she wanted to see me again as soon as possible.

I might be a total fool for agreeing to try this relationship out again, but I've always believed in the saying, "It's better to have lost in love than never to get lost at all." Or something like that. At any rate, I think Jill is worth the risk. It's not like she screwed me over or anything. She just needed to sort things out, and she's obviously arrived at the right decision.

I'm going to be very optimistic about this working out for real this time. Just like I'm optimistic about someday receiving super powers from an advanced alien civilization. Hey, at least one of them is probable, right?

Talk to you later,

Ray Demption

Date: Monday, May 10, 2010
To: Fred Bommerson
From: Jack Woodson
Subject: Dino-Mite!

Hey dude,

I told you, I have no idea why fertilizer was the sale item of choice during my formative years. And yes, I'm going to continue to call it fertilizer, not the four letter expletive that you kept slinging around.

Cerulean is fine, thanks for asking. Her mom had to cough up the money for the bars she ate, and the rest were returned to the office. I don't think Cerulean is going to be going anywhere near chocolate of any sort for quite a while.

Thanks for your support on the matter of Jill. Don't worry, if things work out, as I hope they will, I'll forgive you for calling her a black spork.

Back to school stuff, this afternoon, I was talking with my class about the solar system, and we started discussing asteroids and meteors. I explained to the kids that there is a theory that says that a huge meteor struck the Earth, and this is what caused all of the dinosaurs to die.

Since I have painstakingly taught them the scientific method, this immediately led to fact-finding questions of, "Where are the dinosaurs now?" "Did King Kong live with the dinosaurs?" and, "Did you see Jurassic Park?"

Once we were on the topic of dinosaurs and their ilk, Lance saw fit to share a story about the time he picked up a lizard and put it in his cousin's sandwich. While all of the other kids in the class were making retching sounds, I tried to explain that you should never touch a lizard, or any other wild animal for that matter, because of the diseases they carry. Without actually using the word salmonella, I told the kids that lizards carry a disease that can make your stomach hurt really bad.

A couple of the kids piped up with, "And you can get rabies!!" I agreed with them that rabies is a disease that some animals carry.

Victor then raised his hand and asked, "Do birds give you herpes?"

While the sarcastic side of me wanted to answer, "Yes, and those lousy unicorns will give you genital warts," I instead responded with, "Uhhhhhhhhhh, I don't think so. But I wouldn't chance it."

Since there are only three weeks (and change) of school left, I thought I would stop having a word problem as my bell ringer activity and switch to something more fun. Of course, I suppose I should have remembered that fun is in the brain of the beholder.

I've got a set of overhead transparencies that display logic puzzles. You know the ones – Bozo, Flozo, and Schmozo own a dog, a cat, and a herpes-spreading parakeet. Read these clues and fill in the grid to determine which pet goes with which kid.

Personally, I have always LOVED logic puzzles like this. Of course, I love math also, so call me screwy. When I've done logic puzzles with my third graders in the past, they've enjoyed them as well.

Maybe these kids will grow into them. However, the first day was no reason to celebrate their arrival.

The first puzzle in the set involved three boys – Richie, Howard, and Leo – having their birthday parties at three different places – the swimming pool, the roller rink, and the mini golf course. I showed the kids how they needed to copy the grid that had the boys' names and the place names. We read the first clue together, which said something along the lines of, "Richie and the boy who had his party at the roller rink are best friends."

I then asked the kids, "So what does this clue tell us about Richie or the other boys?"

Several hands went into the air. I called on Betsy, who is one of my brighter girls.

"It tells us that they are very excited about having their birthday parties?"

Hmmm… I hadn't considered that. I replied, "Um, they probably are, but remember we're trying to figure out WHERE each boy is having his party."

Next I called on Amir.

"They are happy?"

OK, I thought, this is not going in the right direction. Maybe if, instead of party locations, the top part of the grid showed emotions like Happy, Excited, and Manic-Depressive, THEN we'd be getting somewhere.

But still I pressed on. "The boys are all happy and excited, but we are looking for a clue to WHERE the boys are having their parties. Let's read the clue again. Richie AND the boy who had his party at the roller rink. What do you think?"

Hillary had her hand raised.

"I think they will have their parties at a house because those places are too expensive."

By this time, I was making "gaga" sounds, flapping my lips with my finger, and rolling my head around in circles. Finally, Thilleenica stepped up and offered the right piece of information from the clue.

Despite the rough first outing, I am determined to stay the course here. I feel strongly that puzzles like this really exercise the brain, and I have some kids whose brains seem to be morbidly obese.

Maybe tomorrow's puzzle should be about animals and the disease each one spreads. That might capture the kids' interest a little better.

Later,

Jude Lawjic

Date: Wednesday, May 12, 2010
To: Fred Bommerson
From: Jack Woodson
Subject: What is that heavenly aroma?

Hey Fred,

I certainly did enjoy your hand-crafted logic puzzle about recent woes there at HPU. Let me see if I interpreted the clues correctly. I'm going to go with Latya getting busted for coming in to work at 11:00 three days in a row; Tiffany leaving a tube of lipstick to melt all over a circuit board; and Larry hitting on the new parts inspector out on the line.

Though those last two really could go either way.

The melted lipstick almost sounds like the beginning of a science project, so it's fitting that that's my topic for today. I am super thankful that this year, we moved the science fair to a date AFTER the TAKS. There have been years when we've had to squeeze in projects while stressing over math review. During those years, I will admit, I was much more lenient and allowed somewhat less than rigorous project ideas.

"OK, class, we have 30 minutes to complete the project, and that's it! If you don't already have an idea, we're going with, 'How many fingers does Mr. Woodson have?' Write down your hypothesis now."

You'd be amazed at how wild and varied the guesses were.

A few weeks ago, we spent a few days doing a sample project together. It was titled, "Which will fly farther: a plain paper airplane or a paper airplane with a paperclip on the nose?"

It was a nice diversion during TAKS review week, the kids had fun, and I got to show them exactly what would be expected on their projects.

At one point, one of my cabinet doors was left open, and Jacob saw the big bottle of ketchup I keep on a shelf (ever since the run-in with the Ketchup Nazi). He pointed to it and asked, "Are we doing a science experiment with that?"

We certainly weren't going to waste perfectly good Heinz on an experiment, but it was good to see that at least some of the kids had their brains in science project mode.

For the weekend right after the TAKS, their homework was to jot down a few ideas for potential projects to explore. I was looking for some open-ended questions and some feeling for what kinds of experiments they were interested in.

I got back a few viable responses, but as usual, the nonviable ones blew them out of the water.

I figured there would be some questions that don't require an experiment to answer. Lakeisha submitted, "What is longer, a ruler or a journal?"

Hey, at least she's exploring, right?

Tyler gave me one that would actually be interesting to see put into motion: "How does a solid change when you hit something with it?"

I can imagine Tyler walking around whacking everything in sight with a backpack, a lunch box, or a baseball bat.

Kevin asked, "How long can a human stay underwater?"

Not a bad question, though I'm not sure how we'd test it here in the classroom. I'm tempted to tell him to revise it to "How long can a third grader stay quiet?"

From the "Let Me Know When You Find the Answer" files, Chassany asked, "How do you think liquid was invented?"

Or maybe it was "How do you think liquor was invented?" – the spelling was a bit hard to make out.

Betsy turned in one of my favorites: "If I stop feeding my turtle for 10 days will it die?"

My hypothesis – the turtle will croak.

Not at all unexpectedly, Eddie took the prize for the most bizarre response:

"Which one will last longer – game or cake?"

We might need a separate science project just to INTERPRET that question!

I (gently) suggested a few other ideas to some of these kids, but for the most part, I've let the kids choose their partners and choose their projects, and today we started doing the experiments in class.

Miles, Tomas, and Jessie are probably going to win first prize. They have three different types of liquid – water, Hawaiian Punch, and Coca-Cola – and they are attempting to determine which liquid will best clean a penny. I've hardly had to help them at all. They have a very sound procedure, and they've kept to it.

Three other boys – Jacob, Nestor, and Franco– needed some class participation to complete their project – "Can you identify an object by its smell?" These three were on the ball and had already brought in their materials early last week. That fact will come into play later in my story.

The boys chose five classmates to serve as test subjects, and one at a time they blindfolded their volunteer then held objects in front of that person's nose, asking them to identify the object by its smell.

Their materials list included:
a bag of Hot Cheetos
a dirty sock
an old tennis shoe
a lime
a small thermos filled with strawberry milk

Sitting on the counter in my room for over a week didn't much affect the cheetos, the sock, the shoe, or the lime. However, it didn't do any good for the strawberry milk.

After the boys had collected their data, we pretty much had a reenactment of that old Saturday Night Live skit where one guy says, "YUUCCCKKKKKK!! This milk is rancid!!!" Then his buddy says, "EWWWWW, that's disgusting! Let me try!!"

All of the kids had to smell the milk, whether they were involved with the project or not. I watched as Ta'varon recoiled in horror and then 30 seconds later shouted, "Let me smell that again!"

Before you even ask, let me answer the question that I know you're curious about:

Of COURSE I smelled the milk myself.

I can only hope that when all these kids went home today, woozy with watery eyes and offline olfactory systems, they told their parents, "It was for science!"

Otherwise, I'm gonna get phone calls.

Smell ya later,

50 Scent

Date:	Friday, May 14, 2010
To:	Fred Bommerson
From:	Jack Woodson
Subject:	Milk. It's what's for dinner.

Hey bud,

Thanks for taking it upon yourself to perform Eddie's "Game or cake?" experiment. Your results sound a bit inconclusive, though. You finished a game of solitaire before finishing a small carrot cake, but you polished off a whole bundt cake before your World of Warcraft session was over. I'm going to need to see a full write-up before I can share this with my class.

I love that you're calling it "Eat some of this!"

Today we finally got to do the thing that you guys assume we do twice a week. We went on our field trip! Four months ago, I never thought this day would get here, but we finally got to leave the school and travel. Our destination was The Science Place, which I'm sure you're familiar with. It's a really cool center with lots of hands-on activities, visual aids, and graphic displays. Everyone there seems to have forgotten (or at least forgiven) the whole "Mayonnaise Incident of '05," so there was no problem buying tickets for our large group.

After the bell rang this morning, we didn't stay long at the school. Mrs. Bird and I took the attendance, collected homework from last night, took care of the kids' water imbalances (moved some out, moved some in), and sent the students who were staying behind to various classrooms around the school. Lex, Joaqim, Marcus, and Priya all lost out on their chance to go with us. Let it be known that No Child Left Behind does NOT apply to field trips.

We filled up three school buses for the journey to The Science Place. Actually, the REST of the third grade packed into the first two buses, while Mrs. Bird and I rode in comfort and luxury with our classes in the third bus. Or as close as one can possibly get to comfort and luxury inside a loud, stinky, graffitied school vehicle.

The Science Place is in Fair Park, right next door to where the Texas State Fair is held every year. When the enormous Ferris wheel came into sight, I heard several kids gasp, "Oooh!! Six Flags!!"

These are no doubt the same kids who shout, "Oooh!! Disney World!!" every time they see a duck.

During the twenty minute ride, I learned that Jessie is a very intense joke teller. He's going to tell you a joke, and you're going to laugh!

His first joke was, "What did the carpet say to the floor?"

I said I didn't know (a lie, by the way), and he finished, "I've got you covered!"

I had barely started to smile when Jessie asked, "Did you get it? Did you get it?"

Far too many jokes followed in this same pattern. In Jessie's mind, if someone doesn't immediately chortle, they must not understand the joke.

In the seat behind Jessie, Felipe was making up his own jokes. "What did one dinosaur say to the other dinosaur? I am bigger than you! Said the bigger dinosaur."

He didn't seem too concerned about whether his seat buddy got the humor or not.

Once we got there, everyone really enjoyed themselves. There were simple machines to try out, sound and light experiments to play with, restrooms to use – it was like Christmas in May.

Over in the "Health and the Human Body" area, there was a full-sized ambulance, with a "trauma patient" in the back. By the time I wandered over to that area, there were about ten kids in the ambulance, packed into every available space around the gurney, and they were all trying to get their hands on the fake heart stimulator paddles. Clearly, some of these kids have been watching old episodes of ER, because they understand that before you can use these paddles, you have to yell, "CLEAR!" at the top of your lungs. What they DON'T seem to comprehend is the true function of those paddles. In their minds, the object is to strike the patient's chest as violently as possible with the paddles. How this could possibly aid the recovery of a human being, I don't understand. But then, I've never really understood the mass appeal of Justin Bieber, either.

Lunch was nice and serene, out on the side lawn. After everyone had eaten, though, we found that we had a problem. When we picked up our lunches from the cafeteria in the morning, we also took three coolers full of milk and juice cartons (no stinky strawberry milk). The cafeteria ladies told us not to bring back any of the milk or juice. When lunch was over, one cooler was still filled to the brim, and the other two were more than half full.

A-ha, I thought to myself. I have a mission.

When I asked the kids who wanted another milk or juice, I only got about eight takers. That wasn't enough to even put a dent in the amount of liquid we had left over. Next, I told the kids that they would really be helping me out, doing me a personal favor, by drinking another milk or juice. To my great surprise, this actually got a lot of response. Pretty soon, the juice was gone and we were down to one cooler, but it was still nearly full, and the kids seemed to be getting lactose intolerant. When I made the discovery that there was a lot more CHOCOLATE milk hidden under a couple of layers of white milk, the kids got motivated again. I can't believe there are so many milksists at my school!

Nevertheless, I was soon standing over a cooler with about ten cartons of regular white milk in it. Big Jack and Fo'lina had each consumed at least four cartons and were swaying on their feet like punch drunk prizefighters. Nobody else was stepping up to finish the job.

Suddenly, I had a brilliant idea. A super-fantastic, genius idea. I reached down into the cooler and pulled out the object I had spied. I held it up over my head and shouted, "Whoever drinks a carton of milk gets a free ice cube!"

The kids closest to the cooler almost got trampled.

All this time, all I needed to do was offer free ice cubes, and my kids would have bent over backwards to learn their lessons? I'll have to remember that for next year.

Talk to you later,

Ben Afflactose

Date: Tuesday, May 18, 2010
To: Fred Bommerson
From: Jack Woodson
Subject: Don't cross the streams

Hey bud,

"Ice cubes are the new Jolly Ranchers"

I like that line. That would look great on a T-shirt.

I'd say Latya tells slightly higher caliber jokes than Jessie (certainly dirtier jokes), but yeah, he does get a little put out if you don't laugh right away. At least Jessie doesn't trail off into a mumble at the end of every punch line.

I was talking to Jill on the phone last night, and she told me that her school had a "Dress as Your Favorite Character from a Book" Day. She went to class yesterday dressed as Alice in Wonderland, and she had students dressed as Harry Potter, Marvin Redpost, and Nancy Drew. I think that Tweedle Dee and Tweedle Dum were implied.

I told her I would have gone as a Stephen King character – teacher Johnny Smith from The Dead Zone. I wouldn't be readily identifiable from my clothing, but I could have fun going around shaking kids' hands and making creepy and eerily accurate prophecies.

"You are going to have a bland hamburger for lunch. You're going to get put in time out at 2:14. You're going to fidget."

I don't think even Johnny Smith would have been able to foresee the events of today, though. Events involving kids who are mere weeks away from being fourth graders yet who insist on acting like kindergarteners.

Today's malfeasance occurred in the boys' bathroom, a well-documented hotspot of foolishness and bad choices. I was standing near the doorways monitoring the kids in the hall, so I did not see what actually happened. I had to go by witness testimony. And never were there three more unreliable witnesses.

Tyler, Eddie, and Amir were the only boys in the bathroom at the time. Tyler and Eddie were the two actually involved in the incident, so they were not inclined to tell the whole truth, and Amir (doesn't like the feel of paper, keeps a wet stick in his backpack) is just so loopy, I never know if I can take him at his word.

Tyler came running out of the restroom to tell me that Eddie had peed on his shoe. Eddie was right behind him, and HE insisted that Tyler had poured some water on his own shoe.

Tyler's shoe was definitely wet, but I wasn't about to get down on all fours and do a taste and smell analysis. Instead, I asked Amir what had happened. According to Amir, here's what really occurred:

Amir and Tyler were standing at the side-by-side urinals when Eddie came in behind them. Rather than do the logical thing and use one of the four empty stalls, Eddie decided to do the next best thing. Move up uncomfortably close to the two boys and threaten to pee on them if they didn't move quickly.

Amir took the threat to heart and vacated his spot, while Tyler chose instead to DARE Eddie to go ahead and pee on him.

Unfortunately, Amir did not actually see whether Eddie took the dare, so I had to ponder the available evidence. On the one hand, Eddie had just threatened to urinate on a fellow student, and I'm fairly confident that he lacks the maturity to turn down a dare. On the other hand, Tyler never said, "Simon says, pee on my foot."

In the end, I found both parties at fault, and "Rover" and "Hydrant" will be spending the next couple of days at their respective homes. Hopefully, with newspaper laid down on the floor.

All in all, we learned two major life lessons today. Lesson #1 – If you do not want someone to pee on your foot, do not DARE them to pee on your foot.

Lesson #2 – One really should not giggle when a student with a heavy Hispanic accent (like Mia) continuously pronounces the word "journal" as "urinal." The first time she said, "I put my urinal in my desk?" I was a little scared, but now I just have to bite my tongue.

It's probably a good thing we didn't do Character Day at my school. Dick and Jane would be fine, but there would have been far too many Spots.

Later,

I. P. Freely

208

Date: Thursday, May 20, 2010
To: Fred Bommerson
From: Jack Woodson
Subject: Who was that masked midget?

Hey man,

I knew you were going to mention that time Larry threatened to pee on your foot. Or those times, I should say. None of them involving a jellyfish sting.

If we did have a Character Day at my school, I would have to think of something a lot more obvious and youth-oriented than what you suggested. I realize that Atlas Shrugged is your favorite book, but if I wore a T-shirt that said, "I am John Galt," NO ONE would get that, including most of the other teachers!

Horrible idea! Just terrible! I don't know why I ever listen to any of your suggestions!

Although your suggestion to get burritos from Freebirds over the weekend was a great one, so forget what I just said.

This morning, Mrs. Fitzgerald called me to say she was running late and to ask if I would get her class started. I quickly got all of my kids into my room, put up a logic puzzle – which they've really taken to, by the way – and then picked up Mrs. Fitzgerald's class. I was down in her room with them for about five minutes until a teacher's assistant came, then I went back to my own classroom.

When I entered my room, the first thing I noticed was that Charles, who had come in late, looked like he had been in a bar fight. He had a black eye and several bruises on his face. Charles is not the brawling type at all, so I was shocked at his appearance. I asked him, "What happened to you??!?" and he replied, in a very matter-of-fact tone, "Oh, I got my butt kicked by a midget."

Now THAT'S something you don't hear every day, Chauncey!

I wasn't going to be fazed, though. He said it so nonchalantly that I figured I should respond in kind. I just said, "Oh, that's cool," as if that was the most commonplace response in the world, then I turned to talk to one of the other children. The whole exchange had taken about four seconds, and in my mind I was wondering, "What. The. Hell????"

I waited until recess to follow up. When I asked him again what had happened, he told me the complete story. Yesterday, he had been at the pool at his apartment, and he had just gotten out and was drying himself off. Some kid, much smaller than him, had come up and said, "You wanna fight?" Charles had shrugged and said, "OK, why not?" Based on his appearance, he had then let the little kid use his face as a punching bag.

I suggested that the next time someone propositioned him with the question, "You wanna fight?" that his answer should be, "No, thank you, I would very much prefer to do something else."

Something even more surreal (surrealer?) happened after recess, when the class was lined up to take their restroom break. As usual, the boys were as close to resembling an orderly line as Ron Philby is to resembling Kareem Abdul Jabbar. Suddenly, I heard Charles say, "Hey, you know those Subway commercials?"

He then started singing the jingle that goes with those Subway commercials.

"Five... Five Dollar... Five Dollar Foot Looooong..."

Then the surrealest moment of all came – all of the other boys in line started singing the jingle along with him! Suddenly I've got this line of ten boys all singing about five dollar foot longs and doing the accompanying hand motions.

I figured that midget must have given Charles a concussion, but did the midget get to ALL the boys in my class?

Moving from surreal to bittersweet, towards the end of the day, we received the results of the TAKS test, and they were pretty much exactly what I had been expecting. I had eight kids that didn't pass the math test. They weren't exactly the eight kids that I had expected, though. Two kids that I didn't think would pass did (nice surprise), and two kids that I thought WOULD pass, did not (not so nice surprise).

Ta'varon missed the passing mark by one question, and Felipe only missed by two. Marcus's score was in the teens – no surprise there.

On the opposite end, Tomas, Betsy, and Thilleenica each achieved a perfect score.

I took a bit of time and called each student individually up to my desk to share with them how they had done. I gave Antonio an entire stack of food coupons. I told Big Jack repeatedly that he had, in fact, done good. I let Chassany stare unabashedly at my hair while I told her she had passed.

When I was done speaking with all of them, Temperance raised her hand and asked, "When we come to school tomorrow, will we be in fourth grade?"

I replied, "Sure, and I will have ascended to Ruler of the Seven Kingdoms."

I didn't really say that, but I did gently let Temperance and the class know that they still had to finish the rest of the third grade year. I didn't mention that Mrs. Bird and I HAD joked earlier in the week about printing up fliers that said, "Last day of school – May 21st."

With only nine days of school left, I have a feeling time will pass pretty quickly. This will definitely be the case if I can find that midget and convince him to beat up the rest of my class!
Talk to you later,

Khan Kust

Date: Tuesday, May 25, 2010
To: Fred Bommerson
From: Jack Woodson
Subject: You want fries with that?

Hey bud,

Charles kept referring to a midget, but it was really a little kid. So it wouldn't be fair to send Philby out to strike terror into the hearts of my students.

Besides, some of them could probably beat Philby up.

Today we had Career Day at the school. Career Day is held annually in the hopes that the kids will see some possibilities for what they can do with their lives. Several representatives of different occupations came to speak throughout the day.

The only mention of a career (other than teaching) that I can remember from this year came last month on one of the TAKS days. I had been sitting by the door of my classroom after school when Ms. Harries, the TAG teacher, walked by with one of the 5th grade ne'er-do-wells. She was haranguing him about something, which came as no surprise to me at all, because when he was in my class two years ago, I was constantly on his case.

Ms. Harries stopped when she saw me and told me to ask this kid what time he had finished his TAKS test. I obliged and asked what time he had finished.

He sullenly replied, "Sometime between 11 and 1."

I looked at him for a long second and then said, "Wow, Troy, you're going to make a fantastic cable repairman someday!"

The presentations today were going on all over the school. Some guests came to specific classrooms, some spoke in the library, and some were outside.

We put both groups of children in Mrs. Bird's room for the first guest, Nurse McCaffrey's husband, who is a lawyer. He talked to the kids about what he does all day – court appearances, studying contracts, etc. The kids were pretty well behaved and asked questions like, "How long did you have to go to school?" "How much money do you make?" and, "Do you like your job?"

Thankfully, no one asked, "Do you like cheese?"

Later in the day, we went out to the street to see some firemen who had brought a ladder truck. The kids were not so attentive to the firemen. While the gentlemen were explaining the dials and gauges on the truck, Eddie suddenly yelled, "LOOK!!" and pointed at a hawk flying overhead.

I wanted to ask the firemen if they could demonstrate the full power of the fire hose by spraying Eddie down.

Mrs. O'Reilly's daughter, Miley, spoke to the entire third grade in the auditorium. She doesn't have a career yet, because she's a college student, but she gave the kids a little taste of what higher education would be like. Every single third grader at my school is now fired up about going to college. Not because Miley told them that they would get to choose their own classes and define their own path. Not because Miley told them that they would be living on their own in a dorm or an apartment. No, what sent these kids into a frenzy was when Miley started talking about campus amenities.

When she said there was a McDonald's on the campus, the kids started cheering wildly. When she mentioned a Pizza Hut that delivered, they went even crazier. The more restaurants she listed, the more insane the kids got. When she said her college had its own bowling alley, I think I saw a kid's head explode.

At the end of the day, all of the third graders went to the library to listen to the manager of a nearby grocery store. He started by briefly explaining his duties, then he fielded questions from the kids. He should have only taken a few questions, because after about three or four, they started getting repetitive.

"Do you have hot dogs at your store?"
"Do you have tuna fish at your store?"
"Do you have lobsters at your store?"

Suzie then woke up from her deep slumber to ask the strangest question of the day. In her slow Southern drawl, making even the smallest words come out with two syllables, she queried, "Is cherries good for you?"

The grocer stared at her for a moment and then moved his gaze up to the ceiling. I think he was looking for hidden cameras to see if he was being Punk'd. Finally, he answered nervously, "Uh, I think all fruits could be said to be good for you."

Suzie nodded happily and then went back to sleep.

When we got back to my classroom, I asked the kids what they wanted to be when they grew up. Several still insisted that they would be basketball players, including Big Jack and Charles, who have a combined vertical leap of a quarter inch.

Strangely enough, no student on Career Day has ever asked me about being a teacher. I would love to be able to tell them that it takes a compassionate heart, an infinite store of patience, and a good friend with whom to exchange sarcastic, ranting emails.

Plus, I live near a Pizza Hut that delivers.

Later,

Oddjob

Date:	Thursday, May 27, 2010
To:	Fred Bommerson
From:	Jack Woodson
Subject:	You are now free to move about the classroom

Hey Fred,

I'm up pretty late writing this, but tomorrow is Friday, and then we have a 3-day weekend, courtesy of Memorial Day!

Every year, you tell me that you would like to come talk to my kids about your job. And every year, I tell you that no one wants to hear about someone sending emails, drinking coffee, and sitting in meetings all day long.

I'm kidding with you. I've really been protecting you all along, keeping you away from sidetracking questions like, "When is your bedtime?" or, "Do you have your own bicycle?"

Next year, though, if you're still interested, I'll let you do it. Just don't blame me if your hair falls out the next day.

This evening was my school's annual International Festival. There are over 60 different countries represented by students and teachers at my school. It's like the UN, except there is much less sharing of the crayons. Everyone went all out to dress festively, prepare native foods, and decorate the halls with the colors and information of many of these countries.

We've spent the entire week preparing and decorating for the festival. This year, the third grade chose China and Ireland as our designated nations. As a result, our hallway is now festooned with construction paper lanterns, pictures of dragons, a giant Blarney Stone sitting next to the Great Wall of China, and several very Asian-looking leprechauns.

Part of the festivities included a food sampling in the cafeteria. We had a limited budget, so we went with Lucky Charms and fortune cookies. They were a huge success.

Going with the fortune cookie motif, I decided to have the kids write some fortunes that we could put up in the hallway and near our table in the cafeteria. As you might expect, I got some interesting submissions.

Here are some of the kids' "fortunes."

"When you are happy your mom is happy."
"One day you will get married and then have a divorce."
"Everyone goes through a lot of phrases."

"If you study and study you will become gooder in school."
"A man with a house does not need another house to give to his children when they are eight years old."
"They say emnesia isn't a word, well here are your lucky numbers 4,8,12,9,6,2,1."

Definitely some pearls of wisdom in there. As well as some opals of confusion, some emeralds of perplexity, and some amethysts of what the hell??

In addition to the hallway decorations and the food, there was a fashion show in the auditorium, with several students dressed in the traditional attire of the countries being represented.

I invited Jill to the festival, and she showed up right as the fashion show was starting. Afterwards, I showed off my classroom and my hallway, and we walked around the basketball court outside where all of the games were set up. The whole time, I could see a roving band of little girls, led by Katie and Ava, following us and giggling.

Then we got to the outrageous part of the evening. I spotted Temperance at a nearby game. She saw Jill and me, waved at us, and shouted, "Mr. Woodson! Is that your mother?"

I could feel my face turning bright red as I thought, "No, you little wing nut! Just like the 13-year-old that just walked by me is not my grandfather!"

I turned, extremely embarrassed, to apologize to Jill, but she was laughing. She saw my embarrassment, took my hand, and whispered in my ear, "It's ok. MY kids probably would have asked if you were my pimp."

Then she kissed me on the cheek, which brought gasps, shouts, and uncontrolled laughing from the group of girls following us.

Spirits buoyed by the warm kiss, I found it in my heart to forgive Temperance's lapse in eyesight and/or good sense. After all, I suppose it's not uncommon for the kids to have a narrow world-view of adults at the school and to see us all as one big family. It's kind of sweet, even.

It's certainly not uncommon, either. Last year, a former student saw me talking with Mr. Redd and asked if we were brothers. Two years ago, when Mrs. Fitzgerald's pregnancy started showing, she told me several times that her kids kept asking her what WE were going to name OUR baby. Heck, Ava has been calling me "Daddy" all year long!

So I'll give Temperance the benefit of the doubt. Just let this serve as a warning, though – stand next to me at your own peril. If my kids see us together, one of them might just think that you birthed me.

Good night,

Oedipus Tex

Date: Thursday, June 3, 2010
To: Fred Bommerson
From: Jack Woodson
Subject: You don't have to go home, but you can't learn
             here

Hey Fred,

Put it in the books, the school year is over! Please collect your money now from everyone who said I wouldn't make it. It was a rough year to be sure, but I have no doubt that with a little relaxation, my grey hair, ulcers, stress rash, and night terrors will disappear in no time.

Thank you for your fortune cookie message, "After countless mistakes, you probably won't screw it up this time with the person you're dating."

Jill is great, and she makes me very happy. I think if we're still together at the end of the lengthy, work-free, wide-open summer break, then we'll probably be in it for the long haul.

School is out, and today was a great close to an eventful year. For the past two days, I've been sending the kids home with overloaded backpacks. They've taken their folders, their journals, their workbooks, their portfolios, and more. I got rid of all the extra homeworks and workbooks that were left over from throughout the year. Still, the kids were clamoring for more! Some of them just like the idea of getting free stuff, so they probably won't do anything with it, but a lot of them told me they were definitely going to play school over the summer.

A few of them, like Hillary and Gloria, started asking for things that I had no intention of sending home.

"Can I have that overhead machine?"
"Can I have Bubba?"

These kids are little Larrys! I flashed back to the time when we were having lunch at a TGIFridays one day, when Larry said to the waiter, "I like your shirt! Can I have it?"

In addition to all of the extra paperwork, I also had a couple of science project boards that had not been claimed yet. The week prior, I had let the kids get together with their science project partners to decide amongst themselves who would take home the project boards. For the most part, the kids were able to come to amicable decisions, and one person from each group took their board home.

As of today, however, I still had two boards from my afternoon class where the group could not decide on who would get it. One group was Ella and Gwenn, and the other was Cerulean and Isabel.

I told these kids that if they couldn't decide, I would cut the boards in half, and each of them would get half of the project. They didn't seem too excited about that, but I told them it was going to be the only fair way to decide.

I pulled out the first board and put the open scissors on either side of the top, preparing to cut. I asked one last time, "Are you sure about this?"

Cerulean cried, "NO! I want to take it home!"

Naturally, Isabel responded, "No, I want it!"

So I started to cut right down the middle. Let me tell you, cutting a science board with a pair of third grade safety scissors is freaking hard!! I could hear a few gasps of horror as I cut. When I finally presented a half to each of the partners, they didn't seem real pleased.

When I pulled out the other board, Ella immediately shrieked, "SHE CAN HAVE IT!!!!"

Ah yes, Old Testament practicality.

We had our end-of-year awards ceremony after lunch, and lots of parents and family came. It was held in the auditorium so the whole third grade could be there together. The teachers each went up to the stage and went through their class lists, announcing one or two awards for each student. Choosing the awards earlier this week presented a bit of a challenge. We were instructed to give every kid at least two awards. For some kids, this was easy. With kids like Tomas, Katie, and Clarisa, I actually had to draw the limit at five or six awards. With other kids, I had to be really creative with the "Teacher's Choice" award. I gave one to Joaqim that read, "Most Consistent," and one to Marcus that said, "Most mobile seating arrangement."

When we got back to the classroom after the awards, I found a note from one of my students from last year. It was written on a salmon-colored piece of paper, folded in half, and it was left taped to my door.

It said, "Hi! Mister Woodson is me Diana. I was in your class in 3rd grade. Now I passed to fifth grade. I'm not going to be here next year I'm going to the new school. Today is my last day of school here. So I'm not to wave to you every time I see you! I'm going to miss you and the 4th grade teachers!"

Very sweet, isn't it? The really funny thing is that her impression of me must have changed dramatically. Last year, on her first day in my class, we could hardly get her to enter the room. She was bawling on my doorstep as her mother and I tried to convince her to come in and sit down at a desk. It finally took Miss Rooker to come and talk her down, in Spanish, before she would even set foot in my room.

With a little time gone by, I guess I turned out to be not so bad after all.

Since we've gone to the dress code, we don't do the end-of-year T-shirt signings anymore. Invariably, there will be a couple of kids walking around in a collared white shirt that has names all over it, but I can't imagine that makes their parents too happy.

Instead, at the end of each class, I gave every kid a big piece of construction paper. I showed them how to fold it repeatedly and draw boxes, and we had an autograph party. The kids collected signatures and notes in the boxes on a medium suitable for framing.

I usually make my own autograph paper as well and get the kids to sign it for me, and it's fun to see what they write. There are always plenty of "Best teacher ever" variations (ticher, techer, tetch), but this group provided a few memorable quotes.

DaQuayvius wrote, "Your best student," which I thought was highly wishful thinking on his part.
Isabel wrote, "You're the teacher I never had," which I found a bit confusing.
Tyler wrote, "Thank you for showing me everything you know."
Nice sentiment, but I'm slightly offended he thinks my knowledge stops at a third grade level.

I signed most of the kids' papers with some variation of "Have a great summer!" Not Lakeisha's, though. Right before she asked me to sign hers, she told me that Lex had written something mean on Ava's paper. So on Lakeisha's paper, I wrote, "Try to work on less tattling over the summer!"

Before we knew it, it was 3:00 and the kids were out the door. Most of them rushed me and gave me a big hug – except Betsy, who shouted, "NO!!" and walked carefully around the group hug.

Once the last child was on a bus and the big yellow transports rolled away, we were left with nothing but the silence of our thoughts. That's when the slow clap began. Started by me. Ignored by everyone else.

Another year has come and gone. My test scores certainly were not the best, but I know everybody got smarter. I got a girlfriend, so the rest is gravy.

Now begins almost three months of rest, relaxation, and recharging the batteries. I've had my eye on those second graders for a while, and something tells me I'm going to need this time off to get ready for them.

I'll also need the time off to get Jill caught up on the entire Star Wars experience.

Over and out,

Brad U Ayshun

Made in the USA
Lexington, KY
15 January 2012